The
Holy
Profane

The Holy Profane

Religion in Black Popular Music

TERESA L. REED

THE UNIVERSITY PRESS OF KENTUCKY

Publication of this volume was made possible in part by
a grant from the National Endowment for the Humanities.

Editorial and Sales Offices: The University Press of Kentucky
663 South Limestone Street, Lexington, Kentucky 40508-4008

07 06 05 04 03   5 4 3 2 1

Library of Congress Cataloging-in-Publication Data
available from the Publisher and from The Library of Congress.

ISBN 0-8131-2255-4

This book is printed on acid-free recycled paper meeting
the requirements of the American National Standard
for Permanence of Paper for Printed Library Materials.

Manufactured in the United States of America

To James

CONTENTS

Preface
ix

Introduction
1

1 Pentecostalism and Black Secular Music
15

2 Blues Lyrics: Voice of Religious Consciousness
39

3 Elder Eatmore and Deacon Jones:
Folk Religion as Humor in Black Secular Recordings
63

4 Rethinking the Devil's Music:
Integration, Religion, and Crossing Over
89

5 Evolution of the Blues Preacher:
Sermonizing Modes in Black Secular Music
113

Postlude: God and Gangsta Rap:
The Theosophy of Tupac Shakur
149

Notes
161

Bibliography
169

Index
175

PREFACE

African Americans have long embraced the notion of a sacred/secular musical dichotomy. That polarization was very much a part of my upbringing in the black, Pentecostal church of my native Gary, Indiana. The strictures of my church background served a twofold purpose: On one hand, the prohibitions against secular music—and secular recreation, in general—ensured that I would be untainted by "the world" and kept, instead, on a solid course toward spiritual growth, and, ultimately, heaven. On the other hand, these religious strictures created a very close-knit community bound together by race, socio-economic status, and our highly conservative shared faith.

My church, Open Door Refuge Church of God in Christ, was founded in a storefront in Gary in the late 1960s. My pastor, Elder Bennett, was a charismatic preacher from Kentucky whose personal claim of faith healing became the basis for the inner-city ministry he established. As were most black, Pentecostal preachers, Elder Bennett was a fervent proponent of faith healing, speaking in tongues, and circumspect living. He was compassionate, stern, and paternalistic, a much-needed father figure for a church composed largely of destitute people from the surrounding ghetto community. His faith, vision, and courage overshadowed his sixth-grade education, and before the end of his life Elder Bennett had built a church, a nursing home, and a school. The influence of his ministry spread far beyond its original ghetto boundaries and became a symbol of hope and progress for African Americans in our community.

This church was the hub of our spiritual, social, and recreational activity. I was not only a student in the church's elementary and grammar school, but, along with my family, I attended worship services several times each week. On Sundays alone there was Sunday School at 10 A.M., followed by a main service at noon, Young Peoples' Willing Workers (another Bible class) at 6 P.M., and an evening service at

8 P.M.. There were also daily prayer services and additional evening services on Tuesday, Friday, and Saturday nights. Needless to say, church occupied more of our lives than virtually anything else.

Such a worship schedule might seem daunting to the outsider, but the fact is we never tired of church. It was there that we could share our joys, our pains, and our testimonies of blessings, big and small. It was at church that we could see the Spirit rouse the tired, the poor, and the elderly from the weightiness and drudgery of their daily lives. As the music filled every corner with electricity, we could watch Mother Myles, dressed in all white, get up and do the holy dance. We could listen to Brother Garnett play the saxophone, hear Sister Turner play the organ, and watch the saints, young and old, clap their hands, beat their tambourines, sing their songs, and get their souls revived. Church was a celebration of community, a place where prayer solved every problem, a place where everyone knew your name.

The church afforded me my first musical experiences. It was in this setting that I sang and played my first solos and decided that I would somehow make music my life's work. There was no shortage of encouragement and feedback for anyone wishing to sing or to play in the service of the Lord, and opportunities to hone one's musical craft were abundant since it seems we were always there. The musicians in my denomination were self-taught amateurs, yet many developed such virtuosity and improvisatory skill that they could rival the most competent of studio professionals. And several of them did. Throughout my young life, I heard whispers about this or that person who had once sung in the church, but was now out there in "the world" performing secular music. These artists were backsliders, defectors from the faith community, fallen from grace. I was in high school when Deniece Williams teamed up with Johnny Mathis on the hit single "Too Much, Too Little, Too Late." Deniece didn't attend my church, but she was a member of my denomination, and she lived in my hometown. Her angelic voice, once the pride of Faith Temple Church of God in Christ, had entered the secular arena, and she was earning more per performance than she could have gotten in a lifetime of freewill offerings. Deniece Williams was castigated for taking up with *worldly music,* but at the same time she was celebrated for achieving the success and stardom about which many of us secretly dreamed.

My musical training in the church was the foundation for my later studies of music in college. I was a freshman when Deniece Williams recorded another hit, "Let's Hear It for the Boy," and a senior when Anita Baker, another church defector, recorded her hit-laden album, *Rapture*. By this time, there was nothing remarkable to me about gospel singers achieving secular fame, as the trend had become commonplace. Furthermore, I no longer believed, as my church background had taught me, that these artists were going to burn in hell.

Nonetheless, questions lingered in my mind as to how the black church, once the most vehement opponent of secular indulgence, could spawn so many celebrated performers of "the Devil's music." Over the years, I've encountered bits and pieces of the answer to this question in books and articles written by scholars interested in various facets of black music. My pursuit of this issue gave rise to still more questions, which I have attempted to address in this book. As a trained music theorist, my natural tendency is to don heavy analytical tools and to study the parameters of music in molecular detail. This work, by contrast, has been driven by the need to resolve an issue close to my heart. My approach has been to listen to music and to write about its messages. In addition, I have consulted both popular and scholarly sources in the fields of religion, communications, African-American history, and American popular culture in order to ground my observations in the appropriate contexts.

I was preparing to write my master's thesis at Tulsa University in Oklahoma when I got the news that Elder Bennett had died. I was unable to travel to Gary to attend his funeral, but the news of his death affected me profoundly and made me pause and consider the deep influence that the church had been in my life. The church not only taught me to love music, but it gave me the experiential basis for exploring questions of music and religion, and it taught me the faith necessary to bring an idea to fruition.

Many contributed to the completion of this work. I must thank my mother and my father, Mr. and Mrs. Lee Shelton, for affording me the spiritual grounding, the discipline, and the freedom to be creative. I thank my husband, James, for unwavering support and encouragement and my family and friends for their positive presence in my life.

In addition, I owe a debt of gratitude to many who assisted with this effort: Marcos Sueiro and Suzanne Flandreau of the Center for Black Music Research; Bruce Nemerov and Mayo Taylor of the Center for Popular Music; Joseph Rivers and John Powell for their critical readings of my work; and Frank Ryan and Tom Horne for demonstrating their commitment to my success.

Finally, many thanks to the following for granting permission to reprint copyrighted works included in this text:

All other lyrics reprinted herein are either in the public domain or in accord with fair use.

INTRODUCTION

The relationship between sacred and secular has been a source of controversy in both the African-American and the West-European musical traditions. For African Americans, however, the sacred/secular duality is relatively new. In the native culture of the first Africans transplanted to the New World, a "non-religious" category of music didn't exist. The influence of Western culture led these Africans to incorporate the sacred/secular dichotomy into their thinking about music. But at the same time they retained the most powerful elements of their African musicality. The result of this hybrid consciousness gave rise to a uniquely African-American approach to the sacred/secular musical distinction.[1]

A thoughtful analysis of African-American culture must begin with a discussion of its West-African roots. Most scholars agree that the diverse cultures of West Africa exhibit a common, unifying worldview distinct from that of the West. The lack of a sacred/secular dichotomy in West-African culture is directly related to the way West Africans experience those elements that in the West are considered spiritual, supernatural, religious, or pertaining to the divine. Unlike the European tradition, in which religion is experienced as rituals performed at appointed times and in designated spaces, West-African religion is much more ubiquitous. Laurenti Magesa describes African religion as "far more than a 'believing way of life' or 'an approach to life' directed by a book. It is a 'way of life' or life itself, where a distinction or separation is not made between religion and other areas of human existence." Africans get their spiritual revelation and inspiration from neither a book nor their oral tradition but from their lives.[2]

1

In traditional West-African culture, the spirit world actively participates in the everyday business of living. Africans recognize the role of the supreme God and the work of various lesser divinities in their daily human existence. In the religion of the Yoruba, for example, the divinity Ésù, whose role is to deceive and instigate mischief, has often been equated with Satan or "the trickster" by Christians and Western anthropologists. The Yoruba themselves, however, see it differently. Noel King states: "There is no dualism in Yoruba tradition, where all is of God. . . . Ésù is the one who knows, who can make known, who can test, try, probe. He is our messenger to the world above, bringing word thence to us. He is everywhere reporting to the divine, organizing morality and piety by any means. . . . He will deceive people into wrong behavior so they may gain favor by their expiation and feed the divinities with their offerings."[3]

Their concept of Ésù is just one example of how the Yoruba experience everyday life in terms of the workings of the divine. The example of Ésù also points out another feature that distinguishes the West-African worldview from that of the West. In the West, religious symbols and rituals—such as the Cross, the Virgin Mary, the Eucharist, and baptism—collectively suggest that the realm of the divine is inherently redemptive and good. For West Africans, however, the realm of the divine is far more comprehensive and includes all dimensions of the supernatural world, both good and evil. Furthermore, they see good and evil as corresponding, even cooperative, realities rather than as opposing forces. Thus, Ésù uses mischief as a way to organize morality.

The West-African notion of the divine is not only comprehensive in that it includes both agents of good and evil, but it also assigns a significant role to the "living dead," or the ancestors. Africans believe their ancestors to be in constant contact with both God and humans, and it is not at all unusual for these spirit beings to intrude into their everyday lives with specific intentions. God, the ancestors, and the spirits all participate in human activity in one way or another. The interaction between the living and the dead, the physical world and the spiritual world, and good and evil suggests that the West-African religious worldview can be described not in terms of bipolar opposites or clear categories but, rather, in terms of blended or even fused dimensions.[4]

Differences between the European and West-African approaches to religion in many ways parallel the differences between the European and West-African approaches to music. In the West, music and the other arts are often approached as objects detached from human experience yet intended for human contemplation and consumption. This perception is evident in the way we in the West talk about music. We speak of music as scores, pieces, cuts, tunes, or tracks rather than in terms of the experience these aural objects afford. At concerts and recitals, protocol demands that we frame our music-objects with appropriate silence before and between pieces. We value precision in performance, and our musical notation leaves little room for variance. Our programs are timed, and our recorded music is measured for duration down to the second. Musical performance in the West is appropriate at designated times and in designated places (i.e., the symphony concert in the orchestra hall), and spatial boundaries separate its participants (i.e., the performer[s] on stage, the listeners in the audience.)[5]

By contrast, traditional West Africans fuse music with everyday life in much the same way that they fuse the divine with everyday life. Unencumbered by spatial and temporal circumscription, music flows freely in all types of settings. Documents from the period of the slave trade describe the omnipresence of music and dancing in West-African societies. Battles, agricultural rites, festivals, political transitions, hunting expeditions, litigation, betrothal, marriage, childbirth, and funerals were all occasions for music-making. Richard Jobson, an English captain sent to West Africa on a trading mission early in the seventeenth century, published one of the earliest descriptions of music in the Gambia River region:

> There is without doubt, no people on the earth more
> naturally affected to the sound of musicke than these
> people; which the principall persons do hold as an orna-
> ment of their state, so as when wee come to see them their
> musicke will seldome be wanting; wherein they have a
> perfect resemblance to the Irish Rimer, sitting in the same

manner as they doe upon the ground, somewhat remote
from the company; and as they use [the] singing of Songs
unto their musicke, the ground and effect whereof is the
rehearsal of the ancient stock of the King, exhalting his
antientry, and recounting over all the worthy and famous
acts by him or them [that] hath been achieved: singing,
likewise *extempore* upon any occasion is offered, whereby
the principall may be pleased; wherein diverse times they
will not forget in our presence to sing in the praise of us
white men, for which he will expect from us some manner
of gratification. Also, if at any time the Kings or principall
persons come unto us trading in the River, they will have
their musicke playing before them, and will follow in order
after their manner, presenting a shew of state.[6]

Generally speaking, traditional West-African music is used to facilitate and intensify life experiences. Its purpose is either to help things
happen or to make things happen. Unlike the European musical object, which is art for its own sake, West-African music is functional.

Music and religion are inextricably bound together in West-African culture, so much so that it is impossible to imagine one without
the other. The specific function of music in African religious ritual is
to facilitate communication with the spirit realm. In order to invoke
the manifestation of specific spirit beings, Africans engage in ritualistic dancing, accompanied by drums and other percussion instruments such as the *ason,* or sacred rattle, and cyclical vocal chanting.
Such rituals encourage the generation of a type of energy or life force
which the Yoruba call *àshe,* and encourage the *orisha,* or lesser divinities, to literally enter and take control of the celebrant's physical
being. This process is commonly referred to as *spirit possession.*

Such rituals are essential to *Vodou,* a complex system of symbols, magic, beliefs, and ceremonies found in West Africa. Vodou
(which comes from the Dahomean word *Vodu,* meaning spirit or God)
was transported from West Africa to the Caribbean Islands (particularly Haiti), Brazil, and the United States via the slave trade. While it
has evolved to exhibit the influence of Western culture and Roman
Catholicism, Vodou remains an essentially West-African religious

form that recognizes the powers and energies that both permeate and emanate from all things, both animate and inanimate. Spirit possession is the primary means through which practitioners of Vodou tap into this power. John Webb, a professor of jazz history who attended a Vodou ceremony as part of his research, notes:

> When one experiences a ceremony, and views the complete materialization of a religion through the music in drumming, singing, dancing, and visual imagery, it is an unforgettable experience. . . . even one drum, vocals, rattle, and dancing can have a mesmerizing and positive effect when performed with the spirituality . . . that was given to us on that memorable day. The complete union of religion, dancing, and music can occur even with a small group.[7]

In the West-African worldview, music is intrinsically spiritual, the sacred is intrinsically musical, and both music and the divine permeate every imaginable part of life. "Scholars seem to agree," says Samuel Floyd, "that the aim of African music has always been to translate the experiences of life and of the spiritual world into sound, enhancing and celebrating life through cradle songs, songs of reflection, historical songs, fertility songs, songs about death and mourning, and other song varieties." It is this conceptual approach to spirituality, coupled with this approach to music, that Africans brought with them to the New World.[8]

Sacred and *secular* were entirely foreign concepts to African slaves arriving in the Colonies. They did not distinguish between music for secular use and music for sacred consumption. The way that slaves used spirituals is evidence of this fact. They did not confine their religious singing to the church, but used the spirituals as rowing songs, field songs, work songs, and social songs.[9]

As African slaves absorbed West European culture they developed the tendency to maintain conceptual boundaries separating the sacred from the profane. To a great extent, this awareness of sacred and secular music resulted from their participation in the European model of worship, which was primarily in the form of church attendance. Slaves attended church in one of three ways: (1) as black members in white congregations, (2) as members of separate black churches with white supervision and leadership, or (3) as black members in all-black churches with black leadership. Although the ultimate trend was toward the third type, all three types maintained a clear line of separation between practices that were either appropriate or inappropriate for church use. In 1899, Jeannette Robinson Murphy, who grew up surrounded by the slaves on her family's plantation, wrote that a slave "was often turned out of church for . . . singing a 'fiddle sing,' which is a secular song, but he could steal all the chickens he wanted and never fall from grace."[10]

Although there were black congregations with black leadership, antebellum conditions precluded the institutionalization of an autonomous black church. Instead, the Christian slaves constituted what some scholars have called the "invisible church," invisible because this church was resident—not in the liturgies or edifices dominated by whites—but in the slaves themselves. Their church attendance notwithstanding, the slaves carried their worship inside of them in much the same way as did their African counterparts. Their African-derived tendency to fuse religion with daily life both coexisted alongside of and transcended the ritual of church attendance. The end of slavery would allow for some degree of reconciliation between the African approach to spirituality and the designation of church as the primary worship place.

At the same time that the invisible black church existed in the slave population of the South, the free black church emerged in the North primarily as denominational spin-offs of their larger, older white counterparts. Although these blacks were free to worship as they chose, their music was heavily criticized. Denouncing the worship practices of black, Methodist Philadelphians in 1819, John F. Watson complained that "one and another of musical feelings, and consonant animal spirits, has been heard stepping the merry strains with all the precision of an avowed *dancer*." Their religious songs drew criticism because they displayed the African aesthetic features of spontaneity, emotional intensity, and dance. To white observers, these practices were intolerable examples of secular behavior.[11]

The transformation of the invisible church into the postbellum visible church was pivotal in the development of African-American consciousness. The former slaves' new freedom to assemble in places designated for worship facilitated the development of a black church culture characterized by its own doctrinal, behavioral, social, and musical norms. Although the church of the former slave population was concentrated primarily in the South and retained the African aesthetic to an even greater degree than the black church in the North, both northern and southern black Christians were influenced by the European belief that sacred and secular music should be kept separate.

The establishment and growth of numerous black churches after the Civil War and toward the end of the nineteenth century occurred against the backdrop of a national religious climate characterized by three connected movements: Evangelicalism, the Holiness movement, and Pentecostalism. Christian Evangelicalism had become the most salient religious movement in American society during the early 1800s. This movement was characterized by its stress upon inward conversion for Christian salvation, and, to that end, it institutionalized the revival as a means for converting sinners and reforming society. Both black and white Evangelicals sought conversion, attended revivals, and viewed their lives in Biblical terms. The revival meeting itself had particular appeal to African Americans since this form of worship grew out of the camp meeting, which was a common type of religious gathering for blacks during slavery.[12]

Generally ardent in their convictions, nineteenth-century Evangelicals took issue with various social institutions and practices that they believed both symptomatic of and responsible for moral decay. Fervent and outspoken, they denounced such institutions as the theater and the opera house, and practices such as dancing, card playing, drinking, and frivolous dress on the grounds that these base amusements interfered with the elevation of the soul.[13] This philosophy was the natural precursor of the movement known as "Wesleyan Sanctification," "Christian Perfectionism," or the "Holiness" movement. Although ideas about sanctification had been in circulation since the mid-1800s, the Holiness movement officially started in 1867 when the "National Camp Meeting Association for the Promotion of Holiness" was organized.[14] The Holiness movement added another dimension to the conversion experience offered by Evangelicalism.

Adherents to Holiness believed that personal conversion was demonstrated by conformity to the moral and behavioral codes that distinguished believers from "the world." In accord with the Evangelical stance, these codes governed matters of dress, recreation, and the like.

The anti-worldly stance of the Holiness movement found further expression in Pentecostalism, a movement born out of the Azusa Street Revival in Los Angeles. Started by William Seymour, this revival attracted many adherents of the Holiness movement who traveled to Azusa Street between 1906 and 1913 to experience the Biblical phenomenon of Holy Spirit baptism with the evidence of *glossolalia,* or what is commonly known as speaking in tongues, a practice first reported in the Bible in the second chapter of Acts.[15]

The philosophies of Evangelicalism, Holiness, and Pentecostalism were so compatible that, even though many Holiness sects actually rejected the practice of glossolalia, the three terms are often used interchangeably. The collective impact of these movements upon African Americans can be seen in the number of black denominations that developed from them around the turn of the century, including the Church of the Living God (1889), The Church of Christ (Holiness) (1907), The National Convention of the Churches of God, Holiness (1914), and the largest of them, The Church of God in Christ (1907).[16]

Although these groups may differ on fine points of doctrine and worship practice, they had a common interest in maintaining a definite distinction between the world and the church, and they used—and to some extent, continue to use—strict behavioral codes to maintain this distinction. In addition to keeping the church separate from the world, however, these codes served another purpose. At a time when they had little, if any, hope of achieving social, political, or economic equality with whites, the adherence to strict religious codes gave many blacks a sense of moral superiority over whites.[17]

Just as the end of the nineteenth century marked the unveiling of the black church and the apex of the Holiness and Pentecostal movements born out of Evangelical Christianity, it also marked a shift in black consciousness from a preoccupation with the afterlife to immediate problems of survival. This shift in consciousness is reflected in the music. The blues became an expressive outlet for blacks dealing with poverty, homelessness, alienation, and the many joys and perils of romantic love. In addition to these secular topics, blues songs frequently made reference to religion. Religion, however, was not the focus of the music. The subjugation of religious themes to secular ones in the blues was disconcerting to older generations of blacks whose most familiar form of song was the Negro spiritual.

Blues singing was first documented in 1901, although it certainly existed well before then.[18] From the time the larger society recognized it as a distinct genre, the music was associated with moral decadence. A 1919 article in *Current Opinion* entitled "Enigmatic Folksongs of the Southern Underworld" characterizes the blues as

> the little songs of the wayward, the impenitent sinners, of the men and women who have lost their way in the world. "Blues" are for the outlaws of society; they are little plaintive or humorous stanzas of irregular rhythm set to music not of the conservatories. When one laments a season in prison one sings "The Jail House Blues." For the girl whose "sweetheart" of the dark alleys has gone otherwhere there are many blues, such as "He Left Me Flat Blues," "Kidded Again Blues," and "A Rat at Heart Blues." The forsaken male has his own repertoire, which includes "Lying Skirt Blues" and "She Done Him Dirt Blues." The loser at craps, the luckless sport ruined by slow horses and fast women, the mourner for rum, the profiteer in things forbidden whom the law has evicted, the sick and lonely woman—all these have their appropriate blues.[19]

The emergence of the blues against the backdrop of the burgeoning black church at the end of the nineteenth century further ensured the recognition of two distinct categories of music: one that was appropriate for church use and one that was not. By the 1920s, black America's approach to the secular category of music is illustrated by the fact that several black blues musicians of the period had double careers in which they sought to appeal to both the sacred and the secular markets of African-American consumers. The popular blues star Blind Lemon Jefferson, for example, recorded "I Want to Be Like Jesus in My Heart" and "All I Want Is That Pure Religion" in 1926 under the pseudonym Deacon L.J. Bates. Other blues musicians who recorded religious music under assumed names were Charlie Patton who became Elder J.J. Handley, and Blind Boy Fuller who became Brother George and His Sanctified Singers.[20]

Perhaps due to the fervent religious climate of the day, sacred recordings actually outsold blues recordings in the late 1920s. The Reverend J.C. Burnett's "The Downfall of Nebuchadnezzar," for example, sold eighty thousand copies, compared to about a quarter of that amount sold of recordings by Bessie Smith.[21] The use of pseudonyms was thus necessary for artists interested in selling records to religious buyers who might object to sacred material by blues singers.

Perhaps no other figure from the early decades of this century exemplifies the distinction, the tension, and the reconciliation of the sacred and the secular in black music more than Thomas Dorsey. Born in 1899 in Villa Rica, Georgia, Dorsey was the son of a minister. While Dorsey's early home life was deeply religious, his coming of age would be somewhat different. Dorsey was an adolescent when he and his family made the transition from rural to urban living. It was as a teenager in Atlanta that Dorsey first flowered as a musician and encountered Ma Rainey and Bessie Smith during his days of "hanging out" at popular black theaters. Using skills he had garnered on his mother's organ, he eventually served as accompanist to both singers and developed a successful blues career that earned him the nickname "Georgia Tom." Despite his success as a bluesman, bouts with depression and family crises kept him returning to the faith of his childhood. It was during these periods of rededication that Dorsey wrote some of the most beloved gospel songs, including the standard "Precious Lord, Take My Hand."

Dorsey ultimately settled in Chicago, and there he fused blues ethos with sacred text to produce what has been called "gospel blues," a genre extremely popular with black urban churchgoers of the 1930s. The implications of Dorsey's musical contribution to the church, in light of his having been a noted blues figure, did not go unnoticed by the establishment of the National Baptist Convention. Michael Harris writes that "although Dorsey may have been converted, he was still a practicing bluesman whose identity as Georgia Tom, one of the most popular blues artists of the time, loomed over that of most old-line ministers. As one notorious for his suggestive blues, Dorsey appeared as a highly visible symbol—beyond and within old line churches—of the literal and figurative lowdownness of blues."[22]

The church's suspicion of Dorsey was not simply a matter of their disapproval of his blues persona. Also at issue was the matter of cultural territoriality. By the 1920s, the older black churches of Chicago had come to be viewed as bastions of cultural refinement and upward mobility, a mobility that, in the minds of many, was best facilitated by embracing highly structured, European-modeled forms of worship and by rejecting the more spontaneous forms of interactive, African-derived folk expression. Harris writes that "old-line ministers . . . specialized in suppressing audience reaction. . . ."[23] The craze that Dorsey caused in religious circles was a threat to the pastor's ability to control the tastes and behaviors—and by extension, the image and respectability—of his congregation.

Nonetheless, Dorsey himself considered the connection between gospel and blues to be self-evident, as the two styles had a similar emotional effect upon its participants. To him, both were equally valid vehicles of feeling, and the nature of the feeling—sacred or secular—was unimportant. He states: "If a woman has lost a man, a man has lost a woman, his feeling reacts to the blues; he feels like expressing it. The same thing acts for a gospel song. Now you're not singing blues; you're singing gospel, good news song, singing about the Creator; but it's the same feeling, a grasping of the heart."[24] Dorsey's gospel blues demonstrates the African tendency to blend dimensions by reconciling the secular to the sacred.

The relationship between secular and sacred elements in black music is a vast and fascinating topic on which many authors have already written. Virtually every noteworthy study of black popular music cites the influence of the black church; conversely, virtually every reputable study of black sacred music cites the influence of secularism. While the sacred/secular issue is a regular feature on the menu of broader discussions about black music, works devoted entirely and exclusively to the issue itself are comparatively few and far between. This small body of literature includes Michael Harris's *The Rise of Gospel Blues: The Music of Thomas Andrew Dorsey in the Urban Church* (1992), Portia Maultsby's article, "The Impact of Gospel Music on the Secular Music Industry" (1992), Jon Michael Spencer's *Blues and Evil* (1993), and Jerma Jackson's dissertation, "Testifying at the Cross: Thomas Andrew Dorsey, Sister Rosetta Tharpe, and the Politics of African-American Sacred and Secular Music" (1995). Of particular interest to me is Spencer's *Blues and Evil*. A scholar of Divinity, Spencer uses theoretical constructs from theology to guide his analysis of evil as conceptualized in blues poetry. In so doing, Spencer paints a picture of black America's religiosity against the backdrop of a particular historical moment.

Like Spencer, I am interested in religion in black secular music, and I have narrowed this study to a probe for the holy within the profane. Unlike Spencer, however, I am anything but a trained theologian, although one might describe me as deeply religious. My work also differs from Spencer's in that my thesis for this study is based more upon my observation of musical norms in the black community than upon academic theory. It is typical, for example, that the black community's most celebrated secular artists have deep roots in the black church. James Brown, Ruth Brown, Sam Cooke, Debarge, Roberta Flack, Aretha Franklin, Marvin Gaye, Whitney Houston, Louis Jordan, B.B. King, Gladys Knight, Tina Turner, Dinah Washington, and Stevie Wonder represent but a fraction of the list of artists who praised, preached, prayed, and shouted in the sanctuary long before they took to the secular stage. This knowledge is the foundation upon which my argument rests, that is, that black secular music conveys the evolving religious consciousness of African Americans in the twentieth century.

The six chapters of my study should be read as closely connected essays rather than as a single, fluid narrative. I devote an entire chapter to the discussion of Pentecostalism specifically because of its salient role in black secular music. Chapter 2 examines blues lyrics, taking an approach opposite to that of Spencer's. Rather than beginning with theoretical ideas, I begin with the lyrics themselves and arrive at conclusions about African-American religious sentiment early in the century. Many of the lyrics in this chapter are presented in their entirety and I approach them at face value, listening carefully to what the poet has to say.

Chapter 3 discusses ways in which black folk religion is satirized and parodied in mid-century black popular music and offers some historical insights into this trend. My fourth chapter explores the important phenomenon of *crossing over* from sacred to secular music in the 1950s as it relates to race, image, politics, and economics during that period. Chapter 5 examines the preacher persona and sermonizing modes in black secular music. Finally, a postlude offers some personal, highly subjective reflections upon the presence of God in so-called gangsta rap.

It is my wish that the reader will ascertain in this book a deeper understanding of the African musical mind, the influence of Westernization, and the powerful connection between the holy and the profane in the black-American psyche.

James Brown (Author's collection)

1

PENTECOSTALISM AND BLACK SECULAR MUSIC

In their book *Stairway to Heaven: The Spiritual Roots of Rock 'n' Roll,* Davin Seay and Mary Neely write that "by the mid fifties, currents of showmanship and sanctification in black American culture were rapidly converging. Whether the glory-bound black Pentecostal preacher was an archetype for James Brown (and every other conked and sweating rhythm and blues hero), or whether it was . . . the other way around hardly seems to matter. They were two sides to the same Janus-faced coin."[1] Indeed, the similarities between rhythm and blues and black Pentecostalism have been well documented. In his performances, James Brown captures the soulful spontaneity of the Sanctified church and the animated exhortation of the Sanctified preacher. He also emulates and incites an emotional intensity parallel to the Holy Spirit possession that is a trademark of the Sanctified worship service. The sounds and gestures common to both Pentecostalism and black secular music, however, result from historical conditions forged well before the 1950s.

The Pentecostal religious tradition is now embraced by many different cultures and Christian denominations. Dating from first-century Christianity and transcending national, cultural, and ethnic boundaries, twentieth-century Pentecostalism has been called one of the watershed phenomena of recent times. In 1995, Pentecostals worldwide were numbered at 410 million.[2] The central tenet of this religious persuasion first appears in the Bible in the second chapter of the Acts of the Apostles: "And when the day of Pentecost was fully come, they were all gathered in one place, in one accord. And there appeared unto them cloven tongues of fire and lighted on each one of them. And they began to speak with tongues, as the Spirit gave them utterance" (Acts 2:1-4). Technically, the practice of "speaking in tongues" or *glossolalia,* is the defining characteristic of Pentecostalism. The term *Pentecostal,* however, has also been used in a broader sense to describe an approach to Christian worship characterized by emotional freedom, intensity, spontaneity, and physical expressivity. In addition to these worship practices, Pentecostals also exhibit the influence of Wesleyan Holiness, the lifestyle patterns of which reflect a more or less literal interpretation of the Bible. For this reason, although they are not synonymous, the terms *Holiness, Sanctified,* and *Pentecostal* are often used interchangeably or in conjunction with each other in many African-American circles.[3]

In the United States, the father of modern-day Pentecostalism is Charles F. Parham, a Bible teacher from Topeka, Kansas. The first and most significant Pentecostal revival of this century was sparked in 1906 by Parham's student William J. Seymour, the son of former slaves. Long before Seymour's Azusa Street revival, however, the worship aesthetic of Pentecostalism was present in the bush meetings and praise houses of the black slaves.

Eyewitness accounts of slave worship practice suggest that these services were characterized by musical improvisation, emotional intensity, dramatic physical expression, and community interaction. Henry Russell's nineteenth-century account of an African-American religious service cites the interplay between minister and congregation, the Africanization of an old psalm tune, and the rhythmic nature of the music. He writes: "When the minister gave out his own version of the Psalm, the choir commenced singing so rapidly that the original tune absolutely ceased to exist—in fact, the fine old psalm tune became thoroughly transformed into a kind of negro melody; and so sudden was the transformation, by accelerating the time, that for a moment, I fancied that not only the choir but the little congregation intended to get up a dance as part of the service."[4] Another description was recorded by John Watson, the nineteenth-century Methodist clergyman who lived in Philadelphia in the early 1800s and reported his observations of African-American religious practices in a work called *Methodist Error or Friendly Christian Advice to Those Methodists Who Indulge in Extravagant Religious Emotions and Bodily Exercises* (Trenton, N.J.: D. and E. Fenton, 1819). In it, he rebukes African-American Methodists for extravagant worship practices and, in the process, vividly describes their approach to religious singing:

> In the blacks' quarter, the coloured people get together, and sing for hours together, short scraps of disjointed affirmations, pledges, or prayers, lengthened out with long repetition choruses. These are all sung in the merry chorus-manner of the southern harvest field, or husking-frolic method, of the slave blacks. . . . With every word so sung, they have a sinking of one or other leg of the body alternately; producing an audible sound of the feet at every step, and as manifest as the steps of actual negro dancing in Virginia. . . . If some, in the meantime sit, they strike the sounds alternately on each thigh. What in the name of religion, can countenance or tolerate such gross perversions of true religion! . . . I have known in some camp meetings, from 50 to 60 people crowded into one tent, after the public devotions had closed, and there continue the whole night, singing tune after tune. . . . Some of these . . . are actually composed as sung, and are indeed almost endless.[5]

Fredrika Bremer, a nineteenth-century novelist, visited the United States from 1849 to 1850 and recorded her observations of a Southern camp meeting in *Homes of the New World: Impressions of America* (New York: Harper and Brothers, 1853). Her account of the tent service includes the following description of black worship style: "In the camp of the blacks is heard a great tumult and a loud cry. Men roar and bawl out; women screech like pigs about to be killed; many, having fallen into convulsions, leap and strike about them, so that they are obliged to be held down. It looks here and there like a regular fight. . . . During all this tumult, the singing continues loud and beautiful, and the thunder joins in with its pealing kettle-drum."[6] In addition to the highly improvisatory singing, a central feature of the African-American worship of the nineteenth century was the shout.

A vivid description of the ring shout appears in the 1867 collection
Slave Songs of the United States. The editor notes:

> The true "shout" takes place on Sundays or on "praise"
> nights through the week, or either in the praise-house or in
> some cabin in which a regular religious meeting has been
> held. Very likely more than half the population of the
> plantation is gathered together. . . . The benches are pushed
> back to the wall when the formal meeting is over, and old
> and young, men and women . . . all stand up in the middle
> of the floor, and when the [spiritual] is struck up, begin
> first walking and by-and-by shuffling round, one after the
> other, in a ring. The foot is hardly taken from the floor, and
> the progression is mainly due to a jerking, hitching motion,
> which agitates the entire shouter, and soon brings out
> streams of perspiration.[7]

Slave narratives are full of anecdotes of the lengths to which slaves
went in order to conceal the sound of their late-night worship. According to many narratives, a common practice was to place an up-
side-down kettle near the door of the cabin to absorb the sound of
singing, clapping, and shouting.[8]

While the African worship aesthetic was pervasive in the antebellum "invisible" black church, approaches to worship would gradually
change as African Americans increasingly assumed denominational
identities. Some black denominations, particularly in the North, would
seek to suppress the dramatic emotional displays so as to achieve a
more structured church service and a more refined image; other denominations, particularly in the South, would continue to encourage
physical expressions of religious ecstasy.

The intensity of the slaves' worship can be attributed, to a great
extent, to their West-African spiritual heritage. Improvisatory singing, energetic dancing, and spirit possession are all part of West-
African religious practice. For white Americans, however, such
behaviors were considered excessive and bizarre. Physical expressions of religious fervor among whites were commonly reported in
the accounts of several small revivals in the United States that are

viewed as significant precursors of twentieth-century Pentecostalism. In 1801, a camp meeting in Cane Ridge, Kentucky, reached its climax with the gathering of twenty-five thousand in search of religious renewal. According to eyewitnesses, the scene was one of "godly hysteria" and included such phenomena as falling, jerking, barking like dogs, falling into trances, the "holy laugh" and "such wild dances as David performed before the Ark of the Lord."[9] Evidence suggests that many whites who engaged in such practices may have been influenced by the African-American example of expressive freedom. In his reprimand of the "chaotic" worship style of black Methodists, John Watson states that their example had "visibly affected the religious manner of some whites."[10]

In addition to the Cane Ridge Revival, a similar revival in 1801 swept the University of Georgia, and students who were eyewitnesses to the revival noted that they heard some of the faithful talk "in unknown tongues."[11] Theirs was one of the earliest reports of glossolalic experience in the United States. In Charles W. Conn's account of an 1896 revival in Cherokee County, North Carolina, he notes that some of the faithful were "curiously exercised by the Holy Spirit" to the extent that they were speaking in unknown languages.[12] A subsequent and much more widely publicized glossolalic manifestation occurred in 1901 in Topeka, Kansas, in a church meeting conducted by Charles F. Parham, who was then director of the Bethel Bible College.

Because he was the first to preach that glossolalia was the only evidence of Holy Spirit baptism, Parham is considered the principal pioneer of modern Pentecostalism. The events of Parham's Topeka revival, however, were but preludes to a much more significant occurrence six years later. It was the revival at the Apostolic Faith Mission on 312 Azusa Street in Los Angeles, California, that generated the Pentecostal explosion whose repercussions are still felt today.

The Apostolic Faith Mission on Azusa Street was the former Stevens African Methodist Episcopal Church, a historical connection that seems symbolic of the centrality of African Americans to the modern Pentecostal movement. The founder and leader of the revival was William Joseph Seymour, a Louisiana native and the son of former slaves.[13] Seymour enrolled in Charles Parham's Bible School, which by 1905 had moved its location to Houston, Texas.

After having embraced Parham's teachings, Seymour left Texas for a preaching engagement in Los Angeles, California, where his first sermon was on Acts 2:4 and the necessity of the glossolalic experience. Although his message was opposed by the Southern California Holiness Association which had sponsored his Los Angeles visit, Seymour continued to preach from porches to an ever-increasing crowd of people gathered in the streets. To accommodate the crowds, he began to hold services in the old Stevens A.M.E. Church building, which by that time was being used as a stable and warehouse. Seymour held his first service there on April 14, 1906, and, for three years following, services were held there three times daily, seven days a week. Aside from the unusual phenomenon of glossolalia at Azusa Street, a noteworthy feature of the revival was the racial integration and cultural diversity represented in its following. As with many smaller revivals of the nineteenth-century camp-meeting tradition, the Azusa revival was racially integrated in an otherwise segregated America. The interracial nature of the revival, however, was viewed with suspicion and disapproval by the larger society, and these sentiments were voiced in the press. H.V. Synan comments that during the revival, it was "reported that . . . 'all the stunts common in old camp meetings among colored folks' were being performed in the services" and that "white people [were] imitating [the] unintelligent, crude negroisms of the Southland."[14] Nonetheless, by the end of 1906, Seymour incorporated his ministry as the Pacific Apostolic Faith Movement and started publication of a periodical, the *Apostolic Faith,* which was circulated to approximately 50,000 subscribers.

The Azusa revival attracted believers from all across the nation and even from overseas, but Seymour's leadership was challenged in 1908 by two of his white office workers, Clara Lum and Florence Crawford. After Seymour rejected Lum's romantic advances, these women stole the mailing list of the *Apostolic Faith* to protest his 1908 marriage to Jenny Moore. In so doing, they destroyed Seymour's ability to communicate with the thousands who considered him their leader. Struggles with other whites reduced Seymour's influence to the point that by 1914 the Azusa Street Mission was a local black church. Seymour died on September 28, 1922.

According to Synan, "Practically every early Pentecostal movement in the world can trace its origins directly or indirectly to Seymour's Azusa Street Mission."[15] Black Americans were particularly affected by the Azusa Street revival, and several founders of the first black Pentecostal denominations were in attendance at the services conducted by Seymour. Charles Harrison Mason, founder of the Church of God in Christ, received his own glossolalic experience during his five-week visit to the Azusa Street Mission.

Just as Seymour's work attracted many blacks to the experience of speaking in tongues, it created a division between blacks who embraced the practice and those who did not. One example of this tension resulted in the formation of the Church of Christ (Holiness) after Charles H. Mason's return from Azusa Street. Mason and Charles Price Jones had both been Holiness preachers and very close friends before the Azusa Revival and had cofounded the Church of God in Christ together in 1896. After Mason embraced glossolalia, however, the two parted ways. Mason's ministry retained the name Church of God in Christ and became the largest African-American Pentecostal denomination in the world; Charles Price Jones founded the non-Pentecostal Church of Christ (Holiness).

Of importance here is that except for the issue of speaking in tongues, many black Holiness denominations founded around the turn of the century are identical in every other way—doctrinally, aesthetically, structurally, and socially—to the black churches that identify themselves as Pentecostal. For this reason, the term *Pentecostal* is often applied to some black churches that don't practice glossolalia, but nevertheless retain the most dramatic elements of the African aesthetic. The term *Holiness/Pentecostal* perhaps more accurately denotes the energetic worship style and Holiness-based moral codes that are common to both groups.

The revivals of the nineteenth century and the Azusa revival of the early 1900s were attractive to African Americans because they institutionalized a concept of spirituality with which blacks had long been familiar. The notion that a divine presence could engender physical responses in human beings was a core component of the West-African belief system, one that persisted in the consciousness of the blacks brought to America. In West Africa, a central component of religious experience is that of spirit possession. It was believed that through ritualistic dancing, the divinities, or the *orisha,* could be summoned to literally enter the physical body of the celebrant. The divinity once "mounted" would then make its presence known by altering the dance with its characteristic gestures. With the goal of spirit possession achieved, the celebrant's intimacy with the Divine is confirmed.[16] Because spirit possession was already a familiar concept to them, blacks could easily accept the notion of possession by the Holy Spirit found in Christianity. Furthermore, they accepted that a natural result of being possessed or filled with the Holy Spirit was some type of physical manifestation, be it shouting, screaming, or speaking in tongues. Thus, for African Americans, the physical dramatics of worship associated with these revivals were not just accepted—they were expected, appreciated, and viewed as evidence of God's proximity.

Charles Harrison Mason was deliberate in his effort to retain the flavor of African slave religion in the worship style of the Church of God in Christ. In the formative years of the denomination, however, black Pentecostals were in conflict about whether to retain or to dispense with traditional slave religious practices such as the shout. This controversy resulted from the desire some blacks had to distance themselves from the stigma and stereotypes of slavery. Mason, however, taught his followers to embrace and celebrate the African expression of their faith, and in his sermons and writings he supported his position with scriptural evidence describing dance as an acceptable form of praise to God.[17]

Generally speaking, black Holiness/Pentecostal churches became easily distinguishable by their successful preservation of several elements of what Ithiel C. Clemmons calls the "African spirit cosmology."[18] These elements include devotional spontaneity, an energetic and improvisatory musical style, a communal, interactive setting, and a Spirit-led approach to temporality. Devotional spontaneity is manifest in the extemporaneous hollers, cries, and handclaps of the faithful. In some cases, individuals may spontaneously speak in tongues. In a black Holiness/Pentecostal church, it is not at all unusual to find the entire congregation—old and young alike—overtaken in the "holy dance" and speaking in tongues. These impromptu expressions are welcome features of the worship experience.

The musicians in these churches are often expert improvisers. They usually play by ear rather than by written music, and their accompaniment of the intensely animated singing, preaching, and shouting is skillfully rendered. Because they must be able to accompany any worshipper singing in any key, the musicians are flexible and creative and may even be described as virtuosic. These churches also incorporate a variety of instruments in their ensembles, the most common of which are piano, Hammond organ, drums, bass and lead guitars, saxophones, and tambourines.

Congregations usually constitute closely knit communities. They address each other as Brother, Sister, and Mother, and they participate collectively in many aspects of the service. Much of the singing is in call-and-response format, and the individual singing as well as the preaching is invariably punctuated with claps, shouts, and other gestures of encouragement from the congregation. Many black Holiness/Pentecostal churches have "nursing guilds" which function specifically to assist, comfort, and, in some cases, help control those overcome with religious ecstasy. For many years, these church nurses have worn the traditional white uniform and cap seen in hospitals. The closeness of these communities results from their frequent church attendance (several times, as opposed to once weekly) and the lifestyle disciplines that set them apart from non-members.

Finally, because the Pentecostal church service is a spirit-led event, beginning and ending times are approximate at best. While there is a loose sense of structure, in general, the preaching starts and ends as the Spirit leads, singing begins and ends as the Spirit leads, and prayer begins and ends as the Spirit leads. A black Pentecostal church service is considered successful and effective only to the extent that the dictates of the Spirit have been observed.

In the years following the Azusa revival, African Americans migrated from the rural South to the urban North in massive numbers. In 1915, many were attracted to northern cities to become part of the wartime labor force.[19] By 1930, 1.2 million blacks had left the South in search of better jobs and living conditions in the industrialized North.[20] The growth of the black church in northern cities during this period reflected these migratory patterns. In particular, Holiness/Pentecostal denominations flourished as they quickly established churches to meet the social and spiritual needs of the growing urban black population. Thus, church growth was not only seen in the expanding membership of existing churches but also in the establishment of many new congregations in homes, rented halls, storefronts, and wherever meetings could be held.

Today, people representing many different nationalities, ethnic backgrounds, and socio-economic classes embrace Pentecostalism. But its first adherents—both in early Christianity and in its twentieth-century form—were drawn from society's underclass. In many ways, William Seymour himself was a prototype of the typical Holiness/Pentecostal believer at the turn of the twentieth century. Like Seymour, most had prior roots in the Holiness movement, and those who embraced glossolalia generally retained their Holiness convictions. Like Seymour, many of those attracted to the revival were either poor or, at most, from the working class. Like Seymour, they were either poorly educated, marginally educated, or, at best, self-taught. Like Seymour, they were predisposed, perhaps due to their common class identity, to more interracial tolerance than the larger society. Similar demographics apply to the developers of jazz and blues at the beginning of the twentieth century.

The flowering of American Pentecostalism around the turn of the century coincides with the most important early developments in black secular music. Although African Americans sang secular tunes during antebellum times, this discussion begins with the styles of the late 1800s and the very beginning of the 1900s, because it was during this era that the precursors of twentieth-century, black popular music emerged.[21] By the late 1800s, a distinctive type of rhythmic syncopation was widely recognized as a defining characteristic of African-American music. Early on, minstrel performers included this syncopation in their caricatured portrayals of black music. In fact, Ernest Hogan, a black minstrel and vaudeville entertainer, published the first piece of sheet music with the label "ragtime." By the time Hogan published "All Coons Look Alike to Me" in 1896, the terms "ragtime" and "ragging" were common descriptors for the distinctive rhythms of black-American secular music and dance. While ragtime is perhaps most widely associated with the piano compositions of Scott Joplin, this style originated in the improvisatory devices of illiterate, black musicians who performed entirely by ear. Additionally, many composers, including Hogan, Bob Cole and J. Rosamond and James Weldon Johnson, and Thomas Turpin, wrote music in the ragtime genre for various vocal and instrumental media in the 1890s and early 1900s.

Along with ragtime, the blues started to gain recognition around the turn of the century. As is the case with ragtime, the exact originator of the blues is unknown. The genre has been described, however, as the postbellum, secular counterpart of the antebellum Negro spiritual. After the Civil War, African Americans throughout the South commonly sang of their daily life struggles and accompanied their singing on harmonicas, guitars, and other homemade musical instruments. Although the blues had undoubtedly been around for quite some time, the earliest documented case of blues singing was in 1901. Ma Rainey, the first to develop a stage career from the genre, reports having first heard the blues sung in 1902.[22]

By the 1910s, the syncopated rhythms of ragtime were incorporated into the highly popular syncopated dance ensemble, one of the most famous of which was James Reese Europe's Clef Club Orchestra. At about the same time that syncopated orchestras introduced the sound of what would be called first "jass" and later "jazz," the first generation of black blues divas was coming of age. These included Ma Rainey, who was most active in the 1910s and 1920s; Mamie Smith, the first black female to be recorded; Ma Rainey's protégé, Bessie Smith, who achieved fame in the 1920s and early 1930s, and several others.

The advent of regular radio programming and the birth of the commercial recording industry in the 1920s brought the first national exposure of black popular music in both its syncopated instrumental form and in its vocal blues form. By the mid-1920s, black-American vernacular music, while immensely popular among the grass roots, was denounced by the conservative element of society as primitive, decadent, and second-rate. The popular magazines and periodicals of the day often featured articles which attempted to critically evaluate and define the role of this new musical craze. One example of such an effort appeared in the August 1924 issue of *Etude* magazine. In it, an article entitled "Where Is Jazz Leading America?" presents a compilation of opinions about the societal role of jazz. (At the time the article was written, it was common to use the terms *jazz* and *ragtime* interchangeably.) Those polled include classically trained American composers, music professors, and orchestral conductors. The opinion of Frank Damrosch, then director of the Institute of Musical Art, encapsulates the sentiments of many in the upper class:

> Jazz is to real music what the caricature is to the portrait.
> The caricature may be clever, but it aims at distortion of
> line and feature in order to make its point; similarly, jazz
> may be clever but its effects are made by exaggeration,
> distortion and vulgarisms. If jazz originated in the dance
> rhythms of the negro, it was at least interesting as the self-
> expression of a primitive race. When jazz was adopted by
> the "highly civilized" white race, it tended to degenerate it
> towards primitivity. When a savage distorts his features and
> paints his face so as to produce startling effects, we smile
> at his childishness; but when a civilized man imitates him,
> not as a joke but in all seriousness, we turn away in disgust.
> Attempts have been made to "elevate" jazz by stealing
> phrases from the classic composers and vulgarizing them
> by the rhythms and devices used in jazz. This is not only an
> outrage on beautiful music, but also a confession of pov-
> erty, of inability to compose music of any value on the part
> of jazz writers. We are living in a state of unrest, of social
> evolution, of transition from a condition of established
> order to a new objective as yet but dimly visualized. This is
> reflected in the jazz fad.[23]

The elite's disdain for jazz, ragtime, and the blues is well documented in this and other articles of the period. In denouncing these popular forms, they typically express two kinds of prejudices: (1) a general bias against the "lower" class of people responsible for generating the music, and (2) a general bias against music in improvisatory rather than notated form. Because the music required none of the literacy valued by the European tradition, the elite were ever suspicious of its authenticity as art.

Ironically, however, by the 1930s, the syncopated dance orchestra of the 1910s and 1920s had evolved into an ensemble that required of its players both musical literacy and improvisational skills. Duke Ellington, Count Basie, and other champions of the big band sound were all trained in music theory and composition and, unlike many of their predecessors who had played entirely by ear, were immortalizing their music in written form. Ellington and other educated jazz musicians were able to gain membership in the American Society of Composers, Authors, and Publishers (ASCAP) and to access its established networks and copyright protection. Thus, they secured the place of jazz as a successful crossover genre with a stable white following.

While jazz players of the 1930s and afterward relied increasingly upon the ability to read music, the typical blues singer neither required nor desired such training. Blues vocalists like Bessie Smith and Charlie Patton retained the pathos of the black rural South and the working class, and by the 1930s Thomas Dorsey's introduction of the blues sound into the religious circuit gave rise to urban gospel, another grassroots form. Dorsey's innovation would make the link between the sound of Bessie Smith's blues and the sound of Mahalia Jackson's gospel undeniable.

Despite their common roots in the vernacular forms of the early 1900s, after the 1930s, jazz and blues would develop separately in terms of performance medium and class association. Jazz would be considered highbrow, primarily instrumental, and crossover; blues, on the other hand, would be considered lowbrow, primarily vocal, and avowedly black. Rhythm and blues would successfully combine elements of both.

In 1949, *Billboard* used the term *rhythm and blues* for the first time to label what had formerly been the race record category. The music to which the term referred, however, had already been popular before it was officially named rhythm and blues. Technically, rhythm and blues is the secular music of black Americans popular from the 1940s to the 1960s. This term, however, can also apply to all of the forms of African-American popular music that since the 1940s have resulted from a synthesis of genres including gospel, big-band, swing, and the blues. Nelson George notes that although it was called "rock

& roll" in the 1950s, "soul" in the 1960s, and "funk," "disco," and "rap" in the 1970s, 1980s, and 1990s, respectively, the crucial elements that underscore the identity of the music have never changed.[24] Since its inception, one of those crucial elements has been its association with black-American secular dance.

An important development in the formative years of rhythm and blues came with the solo career of Louis Jordan. Jordan was a singer and tenor saxophonist who had formerly played in Chick Webb's big band. In 1938, following Webb's death, Jordan formed his own band, the Tympani Five, which included a guitar and fewer horns than the typical big band ensemble. Perhaps the most significant innovation of Jordan's band was the practice of playing the blues at an accelerated tempo. This practice was nicknamed "jumpin' the blues" and the upbeat sound itself was called "jump blues."

Evidence that Jordan was directly influenced by the Pentecostal tradition is very difficult to locate. Whether he intended it to or not, the accelerated tempo of Jordan's jump blues conveyed the energy of Pentecostalism and inspired a host of imitators, including Little Richard and Chuck Berry. Since Little Richard hailed from a Pentecostal background, however, his supposed imitation of Louis Jordan may have been more directly related to his intimate familiarity with the upbeat musical style of the Sanctified church.

Seay and Neely argue convincingly that Pentecostalism was the primary spiritual influence upon the pop music of the 1950s.[25] To support their position, they cite white artists like Elvis Presley and Jerry Lee Lewis and black artists like Little Richard, Sam Cooke, James Brown, and Marvin Gaye, all of whom were reared in the Pentecostal tradition. To this list, one could add B.B. King, whose earliest musical influence was Archie Fair, an older relative who was a guitar-playing, Sanctified preacher, and Tina Turner, who attended the Pentecostal church of a family friend during her childhood. Turner's autobiography contains a description of her childhood involvement with black Pentecostalism. Her sister, Alline, gives the following account of young Anna Mae's behavior at the Sanctified services: "You'd get the Holy Ghost in those services and you'd dance around faster and faster, and the music got louder and louder. One time Ann's underpants fell down around her ankles, she was dancing

Tina Turner (Author's collection)

so hard. But she didn't let up."[26] The hard-driving dance of Tina Turner's stage act is, at times, remarkably similar to what would be seen during a Sanctified service.

The influence of Pentecostalism is particularly salient in secular releases like "Shout!" by the Isley Brothers and "Holy Ghost" by the

B.B. King (Author's collection)

Bar-kays. When the Isley Brothers released "Shout!" in 1959, it became a national hit. This song, which is still popular enough to be
heard in television jingles some forty years later, does more than
mimic Pentecostalism; it *is* Pentecostalism! The performance begins
in true "black preacher" fashion, with the lead Isley sermonizing about

his woman. Overcome with joy, he starts several lines that he can't quite seem to finish: "Now that I got my woman. . . . / Been so good to me, better than I been to myself. . . . / Every time I think about you. . . ." Each phrase prompts an enthusiastic response from the audience until a rhythmic, preacher/congregation call-and-response ensues. After several repetitions of "I gotta get myself ready," the audience is more than primed for the sudden tempo change that comes quickly on the heels of "You know it makes me wanna SHOUT!" At a light-ning fast cut time (half note equals about 176), "SHOUT!" is re-peated (call-and-response style, of course) atop a harmony oscillating between the I and vi chords, and to the accompaniment of handclaps, screams, and hollers. That the shouting is about a woman and not about the Lord hardly detracts from the distinctively Pentecostal emotionalism.

The continued influence of Pentecostalism in the funk era can be seen in "Holy Ghost" by the Bar-kays. Released in 1975 (one of the last recordings issued by Stax), this cut was successful on both the pop and rhythm-and-blues charts:

"Holy Ghost," by the Bar-kays

Holy, Yeah, Yeah, Holy Ghost (Refrain, repeated 4 times)

Girl, your love is like the Holy Ghost
Shakin' all in my bones
I've never felt such a feelin'
In all the days I've been born
Whenever I feel your presence, child
You seem to hypnotize my mind, well
Girl, your love is like the Holy Ghost
I feel like I've been born a second time

(Refrain)

Girl, your love is like the Holy Ghost
The antidote that frees my soul
And no cyclone could ever describe
this feelin' that sets my soul on fire

> You put a runnin' in my walk
> and you put a tremble in my talk
> And this feelin' that I have within
> Said it makes me feel like I've been born again.
> Feel it, feel it,
> feel the spirit
>   (repeats to fade.)

The Isley's "Shout!" shows that in the 1950s and 1960s, the up-tempo sound of Pentecostal "shouting" music was so pervasive in rhythm and blues that very often the only way to distinguish between sacred and secular songs was the lyrics. By the early 1970s, however, the sound of the Holiness shout in secular music was supplanted by the hard driving feel of funk. In fact, "Holy Ghost" sounds nothing like the Pentecostal church, except perhaps at the very beginning of the track when the pitches of a vibrating rubber band evoke the image of an old, country church. In some very poor Holiness congregations, musical instruments were fashioned out of whatever materials were available. One such instrument was made my stretching a string or rubber band over a stick and plucking the "chord" at various points to produce a vibrating pitch. This primitive instrument is an Americanized version of the musical bow, a common instrument in West Africa. The Bar-kays include the sound of the musical bow at the start of the track, but it quickly fades into the characteristic funk groove provided by horns, vocals, synthesizer, and drums.

In comparing his woman's love to the Holy Ghost, the singer gives a vivid, albeit sacrilegious, description of the Pentecostal experience. Phrases like "shakin' all in my bones," and "sets my soul on fire" are the same ones Pentecostals use to describe their religious ecstasy; "runnin' in my walk," is a direct reference to the holy dance, and "tremble in my talk," refers specifically to glossolalia. The lead singer punctuates each line with phrases typical of charismatic, black preaching ("Oh Yeah!" "Well!") with all the conviction of a fresh convert. In "Holy Ghost," the description of the Pentecostal experience is so detailed that one wonders whether the Bar-kays were themselves backslidden members of some Holiness church.

Instrumentalists also incorporated the sounds of the Sanctified church into rhythm and blues. Studio drummer David "Panama" Francis, for example, played in a rhythmic style associated with that of the Pentecostal church on several rhythm-and-blues recordings. Francis used the Church of God in Christ's "common meter" (12/8 and the triplet pattern associated with it) in Screaming Jay Hawkins's "I Put a Spell on You" (1956) and LaVern Baker's "See See Rider" (1962).[27] Many other artists who had intimate familiarity with the ethos of the Pentecostal worship style were inclined to incorporate, to varying degrees, that ethos into their secular artistry.

Later generations of black secular artists would also include several who had been reared in the Holiness/Pentecostal tradition. Deniece Williams, for example, grew up in her uncle's Faith Temple Church of God in Christ in East Chicago, Indiana, and the Debarge family grew up singing in the Bethel Pentecostal Church in Grand Rapids, Michigan, where their uncle was pastor.[28]

Black secular music has incorporated sounds from many sectors of the black church, and the contributions of artists from other denominations figure significantly into its aesthetic. Baptist artists Aretha Franklin, Gladys Knight, and Patti Labelle, for example, are noted for their secular presentations of the gospel sound. The specific contribution of black Pentecostalism, however, was that it specialized in preserving the ritual of spirit possession and the whole collection of African rhythms, sounds, and gestures associated with it. In addition, black Holiness/Pentecostal churches, to a greater degree than others, also approached music not simply as an avenue for devotional expression, but also as a means for inciting spirit possession. In particular, the shout was accompanied by a feel and style of music that marked rhythm and blues and its descendant forms. While many black churches actively sought to quench fiery emotionalism, Holiness/Pentecostal groups actively sought the exact opposite. Rhythm-and-blues artists adapted this approach to secular music, and, as the stage became an analog of the pulpit and the audience an analog of the congregation, these artists measured their effectiveness in direct proportion to the degree of emotional abandon they could incite. It is no wonder then that the culmination of a James Brown performance is that point at which both he and his audience are completely overwhelmed with emotion.

The salience of Pentecostal features in black secular music as well as the number of major artists with Pentecostal roots may seem to suggest that Sanctified singers, musicians, and preachers provided an archetype for rhythm and blues. To some extent, this may be the case. It is equally true, however, that the black Pentecostal church was receptive to secular musical influences. Jazz and the blues both emerged as popular forms just on the heels of the Azusa revival. It is reasonable to assume, therefore, that some of the converts to Pentecostalism had been singers and musicians in these secular venues before joining the Sanctified church. Unlike the Baptists and Methodists who had an older and more established musical tradition, the black Pentecostals had no such tradition and were thus more open to including a variety of instruments in their worship service. Explaining that this attitude continues to be prevalent in Pentecostal thinking, Harvey Cox notes that "most Pentecostals gladly welcome any instrument you can blow, pluck, bow, bang, scrape, or rattle in the praise of God." Cox claims to have seen photos of saxophones being played at Pentecostal revivals as early as 1910.[29] In her dissertation, "Testifying at the Cross: Thomas Andrew Dorsey, Sister Rosetta Tharpe, and the Politics of African-American Sacred and Secular Music," Jerma Jackson also notes that while other denominations considered the guitar a sinful, decadent instrument, "members of the Church of God in Christ, along with other Holiness and Pentecostal denominations, rejected the middle class perception that religion was synonymous with restraint. These mostly working class men and women insisted that religion was a corporeal and emotional experience. They stressed that music was a way of giving praise and, as a result, assigned a religious meaning to upbeat rhythms whether generated from guitars, pianos, or tambourines."[30] The singer/guitarist Rosetta Tharpe was one of several artists who enjoyed crossover success at both the Harlem Church of God in Christ and the Cotton Club. Other artists had secular careers in jazz and blues before devoting their musical talents to the Holiness/Pentecostal church. Robert "Keghouse" Wilkins (b. 1896) was a blues guitarist whose career went as far back as the days of minstrelsy and vaudeville before becoming an ordained minister of the Church of God in Christ in 1950. Arnold "Gatemouth" Moore (b. 1913) was a blues singer with numerous minstrel troupes, carnivals, and big bands before becoming an ordained minister of the Church of God in Christ in 1948. Guitarist/pianist Blind James Brewer (b. 1921) vacillated between music ministry with the Church of God in Christ and Chicago nightclub gigs throughout his life. The Pentecostal church was perhaps as receptive to the influence of secular musical styles as rhythm and blues and other genres were to the influence of the Pentecostal worship aesthetic.

A chronology of the years surrounding the turn of the century reveals that some of the most pivotal events in the black Holiness/Pentecostal tradition and in the black secular music industry occurred almost simultaneously. In 1899, for example, Scott Joplin published his first rag compositions; also in 1899, Charles Harrison Mason and Charles Price Jones were expelled from the Baptist church for their Holiness stance and defense of slave worship practice.[31] In 1909, the Azusa revival ended and W.C. Handy composed "Memphis Blues." In 1914, ASCAP was founded, Handy published "St. Louis Blues," and white ministers withdrew from the formerly interracial Church of God in Christ to form a separate Pentecostal organization, the Assemblies of God.[32] In 1922, the first recordings of a black jazz band as an instrumental ensemble were made in Los Angeles.[33] Also in 1922, William J. Seymour died.

The development and expansion of both black Pentecostalism and rhythm and blues depended largely upon the migration of blacks from the South to the North and from the country to the city. As black Southerners reached the North, so did the Pentecostal church, in order to provide spiritual and social assistance. By the time of Charles Harrison Mason's death in 1961, the Church of God in Christ had evolved into a primarily urban church. As early as 1912, Mason had already begun to send preachers and missionaries to Kansas City, St. Louis, Chicago, New York, Los Angeles, and San Francisco. He also sent workers to establish churches to serve blacks who had left rural areas for urban areas in the South.[34] Meanwhile, wartime migration of black GIs, as well as the mass migration of blacks in search of better living conditions, exposed the larger society to the regional sounds that made up rhythm and blues. This exposure helped to create a national appetite for the music that was both satisfied and reinforced by radio and the record industry.

Because of its youth and relatively liberal climate, Los Angeles provided a mecca common to both rhythm and blues and black Pentecostalism. It was not only the site of the Azusa revival, but also the place where the first jazz band recordings were made and where the majority of the first rhythm-and-blues labels were established. Both William Seymour and Louis Jordan died and were buried in Los Angeles.

The attitudinal climate of Los Angeles was—and is—perhaps more conducive than other places to social "experiments" like the multiracial makeup of the original Azusa Street devotees. Even after the integrated congregations dispersed and reverted to segregated worship, however, Azusa would continue to have far-reaching implications for interracial and intercultural contact and exposure in the United States. First, the Azusa revival provided documentable proof that there could be a peaceful, meaningful, and egalitarian coexistence between blacks and whites. However short-lived, their interracial experience at Azusa left many blacks with the indelible persuasion that divine intervention should and could effect the social changes that were the objects of later civil rights movements. Although many segments of the black church contributed to the success of the Civil Rights Movement of the 1950s and 1960s, the fact that Martin Luther King Jr. gave his last speech at the Mason Temple Church of God in Christ seems to bring the Pentecostal example of racial harmony full circle. Secondly, Azusa exposed thousands of white Americans to the expressive freedom and African aesthetic of black worship and religious music. Because many white believers received this exposure within the context of an event that they believed to be divinely orchestrated, they were not only receptive to these elements of black culture, but they also emulated them and helped to disseminate them throughout the United States.

The interracial contact between lower- and working-class blacks and whites in both the nineteenth-century camp-meeting tradition and at the Azusa Street revival of 1906 may be said to foreshadow the interracial contact between lower- and working-class blacks and whites in the music that came to be called rhythm and blues. On one hand, this contact can be described in terms of profit-driven whites exploiting gullible black artists; on the other hand, however, both the earlier black secular styles and the development of rhythm and blues created a genuine desire in both blacks and whites for a cooperative cultural/recreational experience in a way seldom seen before. Early white jazz and blues artists received harsh criticism and scathing rebuke for singing and playing "the music of the Negro" in much the same way that white worshippers where ostracized for incorporating blatant Africanisms into their religion. Louis Jordan, described by Nelson George as "a natural crossover artist," claimed to have profited as much from white audiences as from black audiences.[35] And Johnny Otis, born in 1921, is the quintessential example of a white rhythm-and-blues artist completely absorbed in African-American culture.

Each in its own way, both black Pentecostalism and the secular music industry offered a haven of self-respect and an avenue for transcendence. In the close-knit community of the Holiness/Pentecostal church, otherwise down-and-out blacks could find meaning and significance. They were free to let loose and they could count on the encouragement of others to do so. And Holy Spirit possession offered them an ecstasy that could be neither orchestrated nor controlled by societal conditions.

In the secular music arena, however, the transcendence was more tangible. However perilous and corrupt it may have been, the recording industry was, to many blacks, an invitation to an unprecedented upward mobility. While the industry produced more casualties than successes, black-American contributions and achievements—both economically and artistically—were still groundbreaking by mid-century standards. In 1957, for example, of all the artists on the year-end pop charts, 29 percent were black.[36]

The aesthetic similarities between black Pentecostalism and black secular music should be understood not in terms of a simple archetype/copy model but in terms of mutual exchange. The secular sound of jazz influenced the music of the Pentecostal church long before the sounds and gestures of the church emerged in rhythm and blues. Although it seems impossible to determine whether the influence of one outweighed the other, the fact remains that the lines between sacred and secular were permanently blurred.

In addition to their aesthetic similarities, the historical, geographical, and social parallels between Pentecostalism and black secular music suggest that these two cultural expressions were both outgrowths of a larger phenomenon. That phenomenon may be characterized, in a very broad sense, as the emergence of African-American cultural identity. The turn of the twentieth century was significant for African Americans because it marked the generational divider between black former slaves and their adult children. Unfamiliar with the constraints of their parents' generation, these adults could assert and celebrate aspects of their culture with an authenticity whose appeal transcended the traditional societal norms. While this discussion cites a particular connection between the Pentecostal movement and the black secular music industry, the years framing the turn of the century and the First World War also contain the seeds of the Harlem Renaissance and the modern Civil Rights Movement. It seems reasonable to suggest, then, that black Pentecostalism and black secular music were more than two sides to the same coin, as Seay and Neely argue. Instead, they were two utterances of a fresh and multifaceted African-American voice.

2

BLUES LYRICS

Voice of Religious Consciousness

In the early 1900s, blues singing was associated with the brothel, the juke joint, and the dregs of black-American society. Whites thus labeled the blues primitive and detestable, while conservative, church-going blacks called it "the Devil's music." Unlike the revered and celebrated Negro spiritual of the nineteenth century, the blues spoke in first person of raw, uncensored, real-life experiences. In its lyrics, subjects like sex, drunkenness, poverty, suicide, violence, and hatred are treated with striking straightforwardness. The defiant, assertive tone of the music is that of a generation of blacks born after slavery and coming of age on the threshold of the twentieth century.

Despite the scandalous nature of the music, religious commentary is salient in the blues text. This religious content has received little attention, however, perhaps because of the music's blatantly "worldly" emphasis. Yet, these lyrics treat religion in a way that yields two important kinds of information: First, it shows how turn-of-the-century blacks integrated secular thought with sacred. In the case of the blues, religious themes, concepts, and images offered resources for creative expression. In fact, familiarity with a uniquely black-American religious perspective is a prerequisite to understanding the many levels of signification in blues poetry.

Secondly, the references to religion in blues lyrics show a gradual yet significant occurrence in African-American history—the postbellum shift in black-American religious consciousness. In this transformation, black religious thought becomes less focused upon the afterlife and the intangible world, and more concerned with the concrete realities of day-to-day living. For the slave, religion and religious institutions allowed for spiritual freedom in lieu of physical freedom. Christianity, with its emphasis on judgment day, heaven's many mansions, and "that great gettin' up mornin'" afforded the slave an alternative focus when his immediate reality was unbearable. In addition, rituals and beliefs derived from West-African spirituality gave slaves a way to make sense out of their otherwise irrational and uncontrollable world. Christianity coupled with West-African spirituality thus made for a potent coping mechanism. For the generations of blacks born after slavery, however, life was both more promising and more complex than it had been before. Faced with different social and survival issues, young black Americans began to rethink the role, relevance, and functionality of religion as it had been passed down to them by their parents and grandparents. Many blues texts convey aspects of this contemplation in a way that few historical documents can.

The origins of individual blues texts are often dubious at best or anonymous at worst. We do know that the blues poem originated in the collective experiences of post-slavery African Americans coming of age during the early 1900s. While discographies give information as to when, where, and by what label and artist a particular song may have been recorded, they often cannot say with specificity who the *original* author of the blues text was. It was also common for blues texts to be revised with each recording or performance and for their individual lines to be fragmented, varied, and re-rhymed. Despite this constant metamorphosis, however, the blues texts serve a cathartic function and reflect genuine, gut-level sentiments of turn-of-the-century black Americans. The texts, in all their crudeness, became the voice of millions who would have otherwise gone unheard.

Although religion is the focus of this discussion, the issue of sexuality is certainly the most conspicuous and pervasive theme in blues lyrics. More often than not, the poet speaks of love gone awry. The predominance of this subject reflects the change in black social life following the slave era. Blacks coming of age after slavery had the freedom to make sexual choices to an extent completely unfamiliar to older generations. The power to pursue romantic partnerships and to exercise some control over the longevity of those relationships brought with it a fair amount of both heartache and exhilaration, as countless blues songs convey. For many blacks, romance functioned in much the same way as religion, meeting emotional needs in an immediate and tangible way. And in some cases, the blues text presents romantic intimacy as the preferred alternative to religion, as Blind Willie McTell's "Broke Down Engine," recorded in New York in 1933, makes clear:

"Broke Down Engine," by Blind Willie McTell

Feel like a broke down engine; mama ain't got no driving-wheel
You ever been down and lonesome; you know just how Willie
   McTell feels
I been shooting craps and gambling; good gal and I done got
   broke
I done pawned my thirty-two special; good gal and my clothes in
   soak
I even went to my praying ground; dropped down on bended knees
I ain't crying for no religion; Lordy give me back my good gal
   please

"Broke Down Engine" is one of many songs that emphasizes the emotional connection between sex and salvation in the mind of the blues artist.

The lyrics included in this chapter are all transcribed from recordings made in the 1920s, 1930s, and early 1940s.[1] I approach each blues poem as though the recording artist him or herself is the author of the text. I do this knowing full well that Joe Williams, for example, may not actually be the original author of the lyrics to "Mr. Devil Blues" and that aspects of his rendition may be borrowed from or shared with other texts. Very often, the texts are the voice of an anonymous or hypothetical perspective more than the real feelings and experiences of the performer on the recording. Since my focus is on content rather than on authorship, however, I find it useful to apply the term "poet" in a generic manner in reference to the perspective from which each text is given, be it that of the singer, the lyricist, or of both. This approach recognizes the textual borrowing and sharing and the deeply emotional and improvisatory treatment of song inherent to blues artistry.

Unless otherwise noted, the texts are presented here in their entirety, although repeated lines have been omitted. Occasionally a long dash (————) or a question mark (?) appears in the text to indicate the transcriber's uncertainty about a particular word or phrase. This uncertainty can result from either the age and poor quality of the recording (often, the only surviving documentation of the song's existence) or the dialect of the performer.

Although blues artists flourished primarily in secular venues, their music cannot be considered apart from early twentieth-century African-American culture. The texts examined here articulate both the primacy of religion as well as the changing place of religion during that pivotal period in black history.

Biblical Imagery in the Blues

White teachers of slaves often used the Bible as a reading textbook because they believed that Bible reading would impart moral values and encourage docile behavior. Literacy, however, was not required for exposure to the Bible, since the oral tradition of slaves transmitted its narratives and passages of scripture through sermon, story, and song. It was common for slaves to "Africanize" Biblical text by manipulating and recontextualizing chronology and character; yet, for the most part, essential elements of Biblical narrative remained intact. The Negro spiritual, "Norah, Hist the Windah" (or "Open the Window, Noah") illustrates the slaves' imaginative treatment of Biblical text:

"Norah, Hist the Windah"

Norah, hist the windah
Norah, hist the windah
Norah, hist the windah
Hist the windah let the dove come in
Oh God comman' Brother Norah one day
Oh hist the windah let the dove come in

An' told Brother Norah to build an ark
Hist the windah let the dove come in
Well, the little turtle dove done droop his wing
Oh hist the windah let the dove come in
An' he gone on Zion's Hill to sing·
Hist the windah let the dove come in[2]

This spiritual features dramatic devices that are uniquely African
American. By speaking directly to Noah as though he were present,
the poet removes the Bible character from the mystical past and
places him in the "here and now." In addition, the poet uses his
imagination to embellish the original text. The Biblical account of
Noah and the ark tells of the dove's flight after the flood, but does not
mention the dove's ultimate destination (Genesis 8:12), so the poet
fills in the gap: "An' he gone on Zion's Hill to sing." Like the creators
of spirituals, blues poets often engaged Bible characters in casual,
one-way conversations or connected the characters to their personal
experiences. Blues poets often revised Biblical narratives, sacrific-
ing the integrity and accuracy of the original text in order to con-
struct lines that better served the singer's cathartic needs. The poetic
liberties common to both spirituals and blues texts are consistent with
the West-African artistic view which values function over form.

As did writers of spirituals, blues poets also often used Biblical
imagery to describe feelings of alienation, loneliness, and despair.
Vol Stevens's "Stonewall Blues," recorded in Memphis in 1930, illustrates this device:

"Stonewall Blues," by Vol Stevens

Tell me mailman; I can't get no news
Know by that baby; I'm bound to have those stonewall blues
I called my good gal; my tongue was too weak to talk
Go where she was; but my feet were too weak to walk
Seem like I can hear; my good gal's voice in the air
Said daddy I have a man ——— ; and you have no rights in there
Oh you ever get in jail; boy and you have no friends
Feel just like Daniel; when they throwed him in the lion's den
My good gal wrote a letter; how do you reckon it read

Come home little daddy; your father's might near dead
How can I come home baby; with these tall rock walls over my
    head
Know by that baby; got no one to hold my aching head
Oh where were you; when the clock struck five 'fore day
Down in that old foundry; trying to roll my cares away

Narratives like the one of Daniel in the lion's den (Daniel 6) appealed to blacks because they told of hope in the face of overwhelming odds. As do many Old Testament narratives, the account of Daniel
describes the plight of a nation in captivity, an experience with which
African Americans readily identified. The victim of a cruel injustice,
the poet in "Stonewall Blues" compares himself to Daniel and in so
doing comments on both the unfairness of his imprisonment and the
apparent hopelessness of his situation. But because Daniel was ultimately rescued, the comparison also allows the poet to imply the
view that divine intervention will bring about escape.

The last two lines of the text indirectly refer to the resurrection
of Christ. The New Testament Gospels indicate that Jesus' followers
came to the tomb before daybreak to find that the stone sealing its
entrance had been rolled away (Matthew 28:2). Again, the theme
here is liberation against all odds. The lines, "Oh where were you;
when the clock struck five 'fore day" and "Down in that old foundry;
trying to roll my cares away" clearly invoke two elements of the
story: the time of day and the rolled away stone. Again, by connect-
ing his experience to that of the resurrected Christ, the poet conveys
a subtle, latent optimism.

George Torey's "Lonesome Man Blues," recorded in Birmingham in 1937 and Peter Chatman's "Lend Me Your Love," recorded in
Chicago in 1941, are just two of many blues texts that reference the
story of Noah and the ark: (The excerpt of "Lonesome Man Blues"
begins with line 5.)

"Lonesome Man Blues," by George Torey

Just as sure as a bluebird; flies in the skies above
Say your life ain't no pleasure; unless you with that one you love
Then if I just had wings; then I'd fly just like Noah's dove

Then I would heist my wings; and fly and light on that woman I
   love
Well I went up on a mountain; taking a peep in that old deep blue
   sea
I said I spied that woman; put them things on me
Singing now hey how long; is you going to still do me wrong
Said I woke up this morning; just about the dawn of day
Some man had my woman; and the worried blues had me

"Lend Me Your Love," by Peter Chatman

Now lend me your love; baby, please lend me your love
I know you hear me keep moaning; just like Noah's dove
You got a mortgage on my love; you know there really is no
   doubt
But someday I'm going to find another woman; is going to buy
   your love mortgage out

"Noah's dove" is a popular image in blues poetry, and its use may be
a direct descendent of the well-known spiritual "Norah, Hist the
Windah." These poets use Noah's dove as a symbol of transience and
yearning for emotional freedom, repose, and romantic fulfillment.
The symbol is effective not only because blues singers and their audiences knew the story of Noah and the ark, but because the dove in
the story supplied a subtext that people could connect to their personal experiences. After the flood, Noah sends the dove out to search
for dry land. Released, the dove revels in its freedom, but searches in
desperation for a dry place to rest. The paradox of ostensible freedom and longing for rest was all too familiar to black Americans
struggling for a secure place in American society around the turn of
the century.

   In both texts, the object of the longing is the love of a woman
who refuses him the "rest" he desires, a repose that is both physical and emotional in nature. These texts show how blues poets
use Biblical imagery as metaphors for romantic desire and underscore the intersection between romance and religion in the mind
of the poet.

   While Stevens, Torey, and Chatman sing of romantic longing,

the tone of Kokomo Arnold's "The Twelves," recorded in Chicago in 1935, mixes humor with defiance. The text here begins with the African-American fun-poking tradition of "the dozens" (hence, "The Twelves") and segues into a revision of the Creation story:

"The Twelves," by Kokomo Arnold

Says I want everybody; fall in line
Shake your shimmy; like I'm shaking mine
You shake your shimmy; shake it fast
If you can't shake your shimmy; shake your yas yas yas
Says I am with your mama; out across the field
Slipping and a sliding; just like an automobile
I hollered at your mama; I told her to wait
She slipped away from me; Just like a Cadillac Eight
Say I like your mama; sister too
I did like your papa; but your papa wouldn't do
I met your papa; round the corner the other day
I soon found out; that he was funny that a-way
Says I went out yonder; New Orleans
The wildcat jumped; On the sewing machine
The sewing machine; Sewed so fast
Sewed ninety-nine stitches; up his yas yas yas
Says God made Adam; made him stout
He wasn't satisfied; until he made him a snout
He made him a snout; just as long as a rail
He wasn't satisfied; until he made him a tail
He made him a tail; just to fan the flies
He wasn't satisfied; until he made him some eyes
He made him some eyes; just to look on the grass
He wasn't satisfied; then he made his yas yas yas
He made his yas yas yas; so he couldn't get a trick
He wasn't satisfied; until he made him sick
He made him sick; and then made him well
You know by that; the big boy's coughing in hell

This complicated blues lyric contains several levels of meaning: The "dozens" provides a framework for the narrator to comment on his own bisexuality, commentary that is woven through the clever retelling of the Biblical Creation story. The narrator's bisexuality becomes clear in the lines "Say I like your mama, sister too; I did like your papa, but your papa wouldn't do. . . . I soon found out he was funny that a-way." The "yas yas yas" in the text is a code name for the male sexual organ, to which the narrator refers when, again in coded language, he describes his contraction of venereal disease. To recount the sequence of events that lead to the contraction of the disease, the poet calls upon the Creation story of Genesis. Unlike the original story, in which God creates the animals first and then culminates his work with Adam, the poet reverses this order and suggests that God, starting with Adam, gradually strips away his humanity by adding one, and then another and another animalistic attributes until the man-become-animal is unable to engage in sexual intercourse: "He made his yas yas yas; so he couldn't get a trick." Of interest here is that the poet blames God for creating him with the very tendencies that lead to his ultimate demise: "He made him sick; and then made him well; You know by that; the big boy's coughing in hell." The last lines not only suggest the man's ultimate demise, but also reveal suspicion of an apparently fickle God: "He made him sick; and then made him well." The poet thus manipulates Biblical narrative to give his personal assessment of man's relationship to God. The message—that man is hopelessly vulnerable to the whims of a sadistic God—comes through clearly and undoubtedly voices the sentiments of many early twentieth-century blacks who believed their parents' religion had failed them.

To a remarkable extent, blacks retained their West-African concept of the divine despite their exposure to American religious culture. This understanding of the supernatural recognized a complex pantheon of divinities directing good and evil. As they assimilated Western culture, however, blacks integrated their native religious worldview with Biblical ideology and supplanted their pantheon of divinities with those most pronounced in the scriptures: Jesus, God, the angels, and Satan. References to Satan, or the Devil, occur frequently in blues texts, and Joe Williams's "Mr. Devil Blues" is one example. This song voices a skepticism akin to that seen in "The Twelves." Recorded in Memphis in 1929, it is a revealing commentary on this poet's assessment of the relationship between moral choice and the divine.

"Mr. Devil Blues," by Joe Williams

Good Morning Mr. Devil; I come here to chain you down
Every time I move; you got my rider down
You's a mean old Devil; cause me to weep and moan
Cause me to leave my family; and my happy home
I brought my chain; to lock it around your waist
I don't care woman; who gets all in my way
I wouldn't have been here; had not been for you
Now you got me here now; this old way you do
I was at home; doing very well
Now you got me here now; and I'm catching hell
Now look Mr. Devil; see what you done done
You done wrecked my family; caused me to leave a happy home
I'm going to write a letter now; going to mail it in the air
I'm going to ask Dr. Jesus; if the Devil ever been there

The poet's use of language erases the distance between the earthly and the supernatural. He constructs a casual familiarity with the Devil by addressing him as "Mr." and with Jesus by calling him "Dr." His struggle is with the Devil, who has caused him to leave his family and happy home. Although the poet ascribes a slightly higher status to Jesus by calling him "Dr.," the poet makes no attempt in this text to appeal to Dr. Jesus to cure his moral malady. Instead, his intent is to question Jesus, not through the conventional means of prayer, but through a letter mailed "in the air." The implication here is that regular prayer doesn't work, so God must be approached another way. That he opts to mail the letter "in the air" rather than someplace more specific suggests that his attempt to reach God is random, haphazard, without direction. The last line, "I'm going to ask Dr. Jesus; if the Devil ever been there," implies several things at once. The poet may be wondering whether the Devil has been in the same realm where he assumes Jesus to be (in the air); or he may be wondering whether Jesus, like him, has ever been the victim of the Devil's moral harassment; or the line may be a reference to the Biblical account of Satan's presence in heaven before he and a third of the angels where hurled to the earth as punishment for their mutiny against God (Luke 10:18).

The unfolding of the text makes a powerful statement about the poet's perception of good and evil and the supernatural agents that manage these forces. In the very first line, he addresses the Devil with "Good Morning." The Devil not only occupies the first line of the text, but also the primary place in the poet's daily existence. By contrast, Jesus is mentioned in the very last line of the text. The Devil's character is developed, and he is portrayed as powerful and active. The character of Jesus, however, is not developed and he does not act in the text. The poet engages the Devil in conversation, but he hopes only to reach Jesus through a meandering letter. The text suggests that the Devil is close by ("I brought my chain to lock it around your waist") but that Jesus is out there, somewhere in the air. The poet uses these juxtapositions to suggest that the one he calls "Dr." is difficult to reach, without a cure, and possibly on the same plane as his nemesis. A powerful Devil and a distant God have more to do with the breakup of his home than his own moral choice.

The preceding texts are examples of blues lyrics that incorporate Biblical imagery as a part of their poetic unfolding. Still other texts comment upon the role and the function of the Bible itself. To illustrate, a portion of Blind Willie McTell's "Southern Can Is Mine," recorded in 1931 in Atlanta, is cited below:

"Southern Can Is Mine," by Blind Willie McTell

Now look here mama; let me tell you this
Now if you wants to get crooked; I'm going to give you my fist
You might read from Revelation; back to Genesee
You get crooked; your southern can belong to me
If you go uptown; have me arrested and have me put in jail
Some hot shot got money; come in and go my bail
Soon as I get out; kiss the ground
Your southern can; worth two dollar half a pound
You might take it from the south; you might carry it up north
But understand you can't rule; and either be my boss
Take it from the east; hide it in the west
When I get it mama; your can will see no rest

Well ashes to ashes mama; and sand to sand
Every time I hit you; you think I got a dozen hands

Angry and suspicious, the narrating voice in this text threatens violence against his ostensibly devout woman. Her Bible reading, as
indicated in the line, "you might read from Revelation; back to
Genesee" offers him little assurance that she won't "get crooked."
Of interest here is the tone of the text: It is not one of begging, plead-
ing, and longing, as is the case with many blues texts that treat relationships gone sour. Instead, the tone here is of fury and revenge.
Reading between the lines, it seems that the sanctimonious woman
has given him a reason to doubt her integrity, and her betrayal is the
source of his anger. Driven by his anger, the poet spins an elaborate,
violent plan for gaining control should his lover prove unfaithful.
His desperate need for control is made explicit in the line, "But understand you can't rule; and either be my boss."

On one hand, the text here paints a picture of an angry man, his
suspicions about his woman, and the ominous threat of domestic violence. A subtext, however, becomes clear in the lines, "You might
read from Revelation; back to Genesee" and "But understand you
can't rule; and either be my boss." The reversed order of the books of
the Bible (Genesis is first; Revelation is last) does more than effect a
rhyme with the word "me" in the next line; it is a deliberately sacrilegious expression intended to convey a sense of anger. African Americans had the very complex task of defining their morality within the
context of a politically charged, economically motivated version of
Christianity. This brand of antebellum Christianity had been fashioned by Southern society so as to sanction the very oppression against
which blacks struggled and prayed. In "Southern Can is Mine," the
suspect woman and her hollow rituals of religion represent Americanized Christianity, and the angry lover is a prophetic representa-
tion of a black America seething with an unrest that would erupt
most dramatically in the 1950s and 1960s.

Blues Commentary on the Church

By the turn of the century, the black church had become the moral, social, and political focal point of African-American life. The church consolidated communities, preserved traditions, and shaped codes of behavior and interaction. Heavily influenced by Evangelicalism, the black church also drew clear lines of circumscription around its fold, with conformists on the inside and sinners on the outside. Those on the outside often used the blues to voice their own religious consciousness. Through metaphor, innuendo, satire, and symbolism, blues poets made the church and its traditions the object of contemplation and scrutiny.

The preacher personified the culture and traditions of the black church. On the plantation, he (and occasionally, *she*) invariably assumed a role of authority and leadership among slaves. Whites also recognized and exploited the black preacher's natural leadership ability and his influence upon the slave community. Generally speaking, modern black communities continue to recognize the elevated status of clergymen. Early blues poetry suggests, however, that by the 1920s the traditional reverence of the black preacher was being challenged. Changing perceptions about the moral autonomy of the preacher went hand in hand with the changing times. During the antebellum period, the black preacher was both facilitator and product of the religious mentality that enabled the slaves to remain detached from matters of the present and to be focused, instead, upon the afterlife. The more postbellum blacks dealt with immediate realities, though, the less relevant the vestiges of slave religion and its assumptions and taboos became. The black preacher, once so revered as to remain above scrutiny, was often portrayed in blues lyrics as thoroughly human, fallible, and hypocritical.

The skepticism noted in the preceding lyrics by Arnold, Williams, and McTell is echoed in blues texts that address hypocrisy in the pulpit head-on. An example of such a text is Hi Henry Brown's "Preacher Blues." Recorded in New York in 1932, "Preacher Blues" shares some of its lyrics with an old Southern folksong, "If You Want to Hear a Preacher Cuss." It is one of many blues texts in which the womanizing preacher is the subject of a colorful tale:

"Preacher Blues," by Hi Henry Brown

If you want to hear a preacher curse

Take his bread sweet mama; and save him the crust
Preacher in the pulpit; Bible in his hand
Sister in the corner; crying there's my man
Preacher comes to your house; you ask him to rest his hat
Next thing he want to know; sister where your husband at
Come in here Elder; and shut my door
Want you to preach for me the same text you did night before
See that preacher walking down the street
Fixin' to meddle with every sister he meets
Preacher, preacher you nice and kind
Better not catch you at that house of mine

In this text, the preacher abuses his authority and seduces the women in his flock. For the woman receptive to his advances, "preaching" is a metaphor for sex. Of particular interest is the line, "Come in here Elder; and shut my door." "Elder" is a common title for clergymen in black Holiness/Pentecostal churches, particularly, the Church of God in Christ. Since such churches were known for their rigid moral codes, the message of this text—that even the Pentecostal Elder is a hypocrite—becomes even more pointed. Another important issue regarding black male/female relationships emerges in these lyrics. Slavery prevented black men from functioning in authoritative or protective roles with their women. Since all slaves were the property of the white landowner, any marriage or courtship between black men and women was highly tenuous, if it existed at all. Black men were thus cast into a perpetual state of hopeless rivalry with white men. Brown's text suggests that the black man now has a new rival, this time within his own community and in the form of the popular, charismatic preacher. To make matters worse, the black woman, charmed by the preacher's influence, is a willing participant in the betrayal. The perception put forth in this text goes hand in hand with the observation that women have traditionally outnumbered men in black churches, and, despite this imbalance, men occupy the overwhelming majority of leadership positions. Perhaps Brown's text articulates perceptions about preachers that many black men continue to hold.

An excerpt of Kid Wesley Wilson's "The Gin Done Done It," recorded in New York in 1929, is cited below:

"The Gin Done Done It," by Kid Wesley Wilson

Going to take my gal; to a social dance
But I didn't have no seat; in my pants
Give me four dollars; take me in
I took the four dollars; and I bought some gin
I tore my hair; and I walked the streets
I wanted to whip; everyone I meet
Along came John; who's my best friend
Cut his head; till it was a sin
I shot some craps; to my disgrace
I run everybody; out the place
Dice was loaded; made me sore
I left four hustlers; lying on the floor
I went to church; to do the holy roll
Grabbed me a sister; to convert her soul
Two minutes later; preacher came in
She stopped rollin' with me; started rollin' with him

The black Pentecostal church is referenced again in the last four lines of the excerpt: "I went to church; to do the holy roll." Because of their exuberant, highly physical worship style, Pentecostals were commonly called Holy Rollers. This poet suggests a sexual dimension to the physicality of Pentecostal worship, a semantic convenience since "holy roll" was phonetically similar to "jelly roll," slang for sexual delight. Just as "holy roll" becomes a metaphor for sexual conquest, other religious concepts take on sexual meaning in this text. "Convert her soul" clearly means "to seduce" and the preacher in the text is really a Don Juan. In these four lines, the poet paints a picture of a chaotic, sexually charged church with hypocritical leadership.

As the first twelve lines of the excerpt make clear, this characterization of the church is given from the point of view of an incorrigible alcoholic. In actuality, the black church of the 1920s would hardly have been the place for a reprobate, gin-drinking, dice-throwing outlaw, at least not one who flaunted his sin openly. Church membership would have required him to clean up his act. In "The Gin Done Done It," the poet resolves his dilemma of excommunication: Since his alcoholism prevents him from ascending to the moral standards of the church, he creates a fictitious church on par with his own moral standard, a place of unbridled sexuality rather than a place of worship.

As does "The Gin Done Done It," Frank Stokes's "You Shall," recorded in Chicago in 1927, addresses the hypocrisy of the preacher. Stokes's straightforward discourse on the subject is striking. A portion of that text follows:

"You Shall," by Frank Stokes

Oh well, it's Our Father; who art in heaven
The preacher owed me ten dollars; he paid me seven
Thy kingdom come; thy will be done
If I hadn't took the seven, Lord; I wouldn't have gotten none
Oh well, some folks say; that a preacher won't steal
I caught about eleven; in the watermelon field
Just a-cuttin' and a-slicin'; got to tearing up the vine
They's eatin' and talkin'; most all the time
Oh well you see a preacher; lay behind the log
A hand on the trigger; got his eye on the hog
The hog said mmmm; the gun said zip
jumped on the hog with all his grip

Unlike other texts, which critique the preacher's weakness for women, this one deals with the preacher's greed. The poet characterizes him as a scheming opportunist looking to profit at every possible chance. The poet even borrows a common, racist stereotype: the black man as a watermelon-eating buffoon. In this text, there are eleven of them "a-cuttin' and a-slicin'." The number eleven in the text can be read as a reference to the Twelve Disciples minus Judas, Judas being represented in the poem by the preacher who owed ten dollars but paid only seven. The poet's troping of Biblical text, namely, the opening lines of the Lord's Prayer, adds an element of sarcasm to further clarify the distaste with which he views the preacher.

"Preaching" the Blues

Many guitar-playing bluesmen of the 1920s and 1930s were either partially or entirely devoted to the performance of sacred music. Washington Phillips, Mississippi John Hurt, Blind Gary Davis, Blind Lemon Jefferson and others were widely known for their self-accompanied singing of religious music, singing which often included brief spoken sermonettes between stanzas. (An excellent example of such "sing/preaching" is Blind Gary Davis's "You Got to Go Down.") Even the artists whose recordings were primarily sacred utilized the performance style and medium common to black-American folk singing of the day.

It was common for the Evangelical preacher to share in the folk style of the blues singer in the 1920s and 1930s; The blues lyricist created an outspoken satire on these evangelists when he used their stylings to convey his secular message. Son House's "Preachin' the Blues," Parts 1 and 2, were both recorded in Grafton, Wisconsin, in 1930 and are excellent representations of this device. House's performance of "Preachin' the Blues" imitates the inspirational feel of the self-accompanied preacher.

"Preachin' the Blues," by Son House, Part 1

Oh, I'm going to get me religion; I'm going to join the Baptist church
I'm going to be a Baptist preacher; and I sure won't have to work
Oh, I'm going to preach these blues now; and I want everybody to shout
I'm going to do like a prisoner; I'm going to roll my time on out
Oh up in my room; I bowed down to pray
Say the blues come along; and they drove my spirit away
Oh and I had religion; Lord this very day
But the womens and whiskey; well they would not let me pray
Oh I wish I had me; a heaven of my own
Then I'd give all my women; a long long happy home
Yeah I love my baby; just like I love myself
Well, if she don't have me; she won't have nobody else

Part 1 suggests that religion, at least as symbolized by the Baptist preacher, is tantamount to laziness. The poet even compares his preaching self to a prisoner, one sentenced to a conventional religion that is stymied and ineffective. Toward the end of the text the poet admits his own bondage to the women and whiskey that "would not let me pray." He finally asserts that the solution to his dilemma is neither to repent nor to backslide but to have a heaven of his own.

"Preachin' Blues," by Son House, Part 2

Hey I'm going to fold my arms; I'm going to kneel down in prayer
When I get up; I'm going to see if my preaching suit a man's ear
Now, I met the blues this morning; walking just like a man
I said "good morning blues; now give me your right hand"
Now it ain't nothing now baby; Lord, that's going to worry my
    mind
Oh, I'm satisfied; I got the longest line
Oh I got to stay on the job; I ain't got no time to lose
I swear to God; I got to preach these gospel blues
Oh, I'm going to preach these blues; and choose my seat and sit
    down
When the spirit comes, sisters; I want you to jump straight up
    and down

In Part 2, the poet has resolved his spiritual dilemma and is resigned to preaching the blues. In fact, the blues, now personified, is a member of the poet's church. This becomes clear in the line "now give me your right hand." In the black Baptist tradition, church membership is granted when the preacher extends what is called "the right hand of fellowship." The poet thus creates a parallel between joining the church and his own reconciliation to the blues.

In the line, "I got to stay on the job; I ain't got no time to lose," the narrator contrasts his own enthusiasm for "work" with the laziness of the Baptist preacher that he cites in Part 1. His reference to "gospel blues" in the very next line has several meanings that should be interpreted in historical context. In 1930, the same year that House recorded "Preachin' the Blues," Thomas Dorsey revolutionized church music when his "If You See My Savior" was performed at the National Baptist Convention in Chicago. The new style represented in "If You See My Savior" was then known as the "gospel blues" because it incorporated the secular sound from Dorsey's pre-conversion days as the racy and provocative blues performer Georgia Tom. House was also in the Midwest when he recorded "Preachin' the Blues," and he certainly would have known of Dorsey, both as the moderately famous Georgia Tom and as the converted Baptist music minister. House's satirical reference to the gospel blues is indicative not only of the new swankier style of religious singing but may also relate his suspicions about the authenticity of Dorsey's conversion. Finally, as in Part 1, the text of Part 2 concludes with a reference to the narrator's love for women.

Blues Commentary on the Afterlife and the Intangible World

African Americans embraced a literal interpretation of the Bible and believed the afterlife to be an actual place of hope and consequences for one's behavior on earth. Negro spirituals are replete with references to the afterlife, and the very concept motivated the faithful toward Christian behavior. For slaves, the afterlife offered vindication and recourse in the face of earthly insecurities. Unlike the older generation, descendants of former slaves were far more preoccupied with immediate realities and less so with life after death. Pearl Dickson's "Little Rock Blues," recorded in Memphis in 1927, conveys this perspective as she compares a trip to heaven with another option:

"Little Rock Blues," by Pearl Dickson

I started to heaven; but I changed my mind
But I'm going to Little Rock; where I can have a better time
Yes, when I go to Little Rock; I can go three days without
I tell people there; it's a wonderful town
This is the place where I have long to be
Because where I come from; the mens have mistreated poor me
Oh, I don't know why; they treat me so lowdown and cruel
And if you don't want me baby; you don't have to use me as no
    fool

The first line, "I started to heaven; but I changed my mind," can be read in at least two ways. On the one hand, this line can be construed as "I started to embrace religion," while on the other hand, it can mean "I started to commit suicide and thereby access heaven." Read either way, the narrator makes it clear that a trip to Little Rock is preferred to either piety or suicide.

As is often the case in blues lyrics, the meaning of a particular line may be unclear or, at best, tenuously connected to the rest of the song. In these cases, one might view the seemingly nonsensical line as having been conveniently inserted in order to fashion the rhyme. An example of such an instance is the very loosely rhymed pair "I can go three days with*out*. . . . it's a wonderful t*own*." It is obvious that although "without" and "town" do not rhyme, the author intends to connect their similar vowel sounds.

Another way to view this loosely rhymed pair begins with particular attention to the line, "I can go three days without." As the first in the pair, the narrator gives emphasis to this line as a way to carry forward the theme of the afterlife. In her reference to "three days without," the author seems to create a parallel between herself and other Biblical situations involving three days. Jonah, for example, was in the belly of the whale for three days; Jesus was in the tomb for three days. Like Jonah and Jesus, the blues singer emerges after three days, not from a death experience but, rather, from its alternative (Little Rock) to testify not of its horror but that "it's a wonderful town." In this lyric, the poet references, manipulates, and recontextualizes conventional religious meaning to endow an unrhymed line with complex significance.

Son House's "My Black Mama," recorded in 1930 in Grafton, Wisconsin, also addresses the afterlife. The first six lines and last six lines of the text are quoted below:

"My Black Mama," by Son House

Well black Mama, what's the matter with you today
Ain't satisfactory; don't care what I do
You say a brown skin woman will make a rabbit move to town
Say a jet black woman will make a mule kick his stable down
Yeah it ain't no heaven now; and it ain't no burning hell
Said where I'm going when I die; can't nobody tell.

I got a letter this morning; how do you reckon it read

Oh hurry, hurry; the gal you love is dead
I grabbed my suitcase; I took on up the road
I got there, she was laying on the cooling board
Well, I looked up close; I looked down in her face
Good old gal, got to lay there till judgment day

The most interesting feature of this text is the poet's ambiguity about the afterlife. The opening lines describe the frustration of a man who tries unsuccessfully to please the woman he loves. He resolves his dilemma by considering other women and erasing the consequences of his infidelity: "it ain't no heaven. . . . and it ain't no burning hell." With no heaven or hell to consider, he is free to do as he pleases. But the death of his beloved, described in the last six lines, forces him to consider judgment day.

The afterlife as conveyed in Christian thought was but one element of the intangible world that offered slaves solace in the face of adversity. Another element of the supernatural that was prominent in the religious consciousness of slaves was derived from West-African spirituality. The belief in *signs,* or natural occurrences thought to foreshadow an impending circumstance, was as much a part of the spirituality of slaves as was Christianity. Coupled with the belief in signs was a belief in *hants* (or haunts), the visual manifestation of spirit beings. Slaves passed these beliefs and the superstitious practices that accompanied them along to their descendants, and, to some extent, they continue to be alive and well, particularly in older African-American communities in the South.

By the turn of the century the younger generation was beginning to challenge the old beliefs in signs and hants, and the antiquated, superstitious practices surrounding them. The challenge was expressed in works as grand as Scott Joplin's ragtime opera, *Treemonisha* (1911), and in works as quaint as the blues tune. Ida Cox's "Fogyism" (1928), challenges the belief system of the older generation head-on:

"Fogyism," by Ida Cox

Why do people believe in some old sign
You hear a hoot owl holler; someone is surely dying
Some will break a mirror; bad luck for seven years

And if a black cat crosses them; they break right down in tears
To dream of muddy water; trouble is knocking at your door
Your man is sure to leave you; and never return no more
When your man comes home evil; tell you you are getting old
That's a true sign he got someone else bakin' his jellyroll

In its heyday, the blues would have hardly been considered a source
of information about black religious thought; yet these texts, taken
collectively, convey a powerful message about the role of religion in
the black-American consciousness during the early decades of the
twentieth century. Although the blues caused more than a few scan-
dals with its picturesque treatment of sexual themes, its artists still
relied heavily upon religion and religious concepts and images for
expressive creativity. But religion in these texts is far more than a
creative resource. It is also a subject of contemplation. The blues
poet expresses dissatisfaction with aspects of traditional religion that
fail to answer the poet's need for truth and stability. In the poetry, the
preacher, the church, and the afterlife undergo merciless scrutiny.
The poetry is also used to do what never could be done in church: to
question God and to demand an explanation for the poet's plight.

Despite the changing perceptions of traditional religion conveyed
in blues texts, blues artists are far from atheists. Instead, their lyrics
suggest the centrality of their belief in God and a deeply religious
understanding of themselves and the world around them. The very
fact that they use their poetry to grapple with their spirituality suggests the significance of personal faith. That faith is neither autonomous nor static, but subject to the uncertainties of a society passing
from a post-Reconstruction mindset into the twentieth century. Their
religious thinking is evolutionary, and their music conveys all the
tensions that are a natural and inevitable part of change.

Texas Alexander's "Sittin' on a Log," recorded in San Antonio in
1928, inadvertently summarizes the transition within black religious
consciousness in the early twentieth century:

"Sittin' on a Log," by Texas Alexander

I was sitting on a log; just like a doggone dog
That's the mean old woman; come and crossed my heart

Says I went to the church; and they called on me to pray
I fell down on my knees; and forgot just what to say
Oh Lordy mama; what am I to do
I'm just going to stay right here; wait on something new

The poet has not rejected religion; he has simply forgotten how to practice it. The religion of his past somehow no longer provides for him the answers demanded by his current pain. He senses the changing times and resolves to look to the future, to "wait on something new." And perhaps he finds the "something new" not by remembering what to say but by learning a different prayer altogether.

3

ELDER EATMORE
AND DEACON JONES

Folk Religion as Humor in Black Secular Recordings

In 1961, LaVern Baker's "Saved" reached number seventeen on the rhythm-and-blues charts and number thirty-seven on the pop charts. In this hand-clapping, foot-stomping number, Baker sings tongue-in-cheek about the ecstasy of religious conversion. In one verse she testifies: "I used to smoke, drink, and dance the hoochy coo, but now I'm SAVED!!"; in another, "I used to cuss, fuss, and boogie all night long, but now I'm SAVED!!" This up-tempo, call-and-response tune features a clamorous refrain of Salvation Army bass drum and cymbals supported by a "congregation" of backup singers. Baker flavors the number with the soul-stirring, gospel fervor of a seasoned, sanctified chorister.[1]

With its emphasis on conversion, testimony, and soulful celebration, "Saved" points directly to the worship aesthetic of black folk religion. Even so, the tune is no more likely to be mistaken for sacred music than a comic strip is to be mistaken for classical literature. First of all, Baker herself was hardly a saint; instead, she was a *femme fatale,* one of the first real sex symbols in the world of rhythm and blues. Second, on the "B" side of "Saved" is Baker's performance of "Don Juan," a tune about money and sex, subjects more in line with her sultry image. "Saved" is thus a perfect example of satire, a caricatured portrayal of an African-American religious experience. Written by white songwriters Jerry Leiber and Mike Stoller, "Saved" pokes fun at a church tradition often perceived as marginal, crude, frenetic, and humorous.[2]

"Saved" is an important symbol, representing the dynamics of race, religion, and class in black popular music. It symbolizes the cyclical process in much of black music since the 1930s whereby African-American cultural themes are shaped into songs by white songwriters and handed back to black artists for "authentic" interpretation. Second, "Saved" represents the curious two-way potency of the revivalist/Pentecostal phenomenon: On one hand, Pentecostalism and other revivalist traditions have been noted for their ability to engage blacks and whites in a shared spirituality, a feat realized long before integration was socially acceptable. As early as the eighteenth century, revivals and camp meetings attracted the common folk of both races while the rest of American society remained largely segregated. On the other hand, both mainstream whites and many blacks considered Pentecostals and revivalist types to be socially marginal, a common assessment that comes through clearly in popular songs recorded prior to the advent of Soul music. Finally, "Saved" represents the close of an era in black popular music—an era when it was fashionable and fairly common to find religious caricature as the basis for secular songs performed and recorded by black artists.

From the earliest days of the recording industry until the full bloom of the Civil Rights era, secular artists used not just black Pentecostalism but black religion in general as a source of both direct and implicit humor in their popular songs. Even when the black and white entertainment worlds remained largely segregated, artists of both races seemed to agree that black religion—particularly, Southern-born black religion—was comical. The reasons for this apparent consensus are complex and differ according to racial perspective. The recordings by black artists between the 1910s and 1960s that place black religion in the context of humorous, light-hearted entertainment reveal much about the attitudinal climate of the period. These songs and the artists who performed them tell us much about the intersection of racial, religious, and class perceptions and the changing role of religion in African-American society in the middle of the twentieth century.

Since humor comes in many guises, I should first distinguish between religious wit and religious caricature: An example of the former is Jim Jackson's "I Heard the Voice of a Porkchop," recorded in 1928 in Memphis. The refrain in this song is the line "I heard the voice of a porkchop say come unto me and rest." Substituting only "porkchop" for "Jesus," the tune borrows from the mid-nineteenth-century invitational hymn, "I Heard the Voice of Jesus Say," an oft-cited hymn in the African-American lining-out tradition. The humor in the tune results from a poetic manipulation—the personification of the pork chop. One can read between the lines, however, to see that Jackson's witty distortion of the hymn communicates a sentiment that is a recurring theme in blues poetry of the 1920s and 1930s— the generalized feeling among many blacks that traditional religion had failed to meet their social and material needs. In Jackson's tune, then, it is a pork chop—not Jesus—that gives satisfaction.

Although I cite Jim Jackson's tune because of its striking wit, there are literally hundreds of pre–World War II secular recordings by black artists that incorporate religion to varying degrees. Blues singers both before and throughout the early recording era commonly used their music for religious commentary. Along with serious reflections about God, faith, and eternity, humorous quips about the church, its devotees, and its traditions abound in the blues. For example, Frank Stokes's "You Shall," recorded in 1927, begins "Our Father, Who art in heaven, the preacher owed me ten dollars but only paid seven." It's important to keep in mind that, in general, the earliest recorded blues were black expressions intended for black audiences, although whites profited most from the dissemination of "race" music. Early in the twentieth century, segregation precluded any concept of deliberate crossover comparable to that seen in the 1960s and 1970s. Although black music has always had white consumers (thanks, in part, to people like W.C. Handy, who helped to bridge the gap between the oral and written traditions), it was initially targeted squarely at the black consumer market, and there was little, if any, effort to tailor the blues to white taste or comprehension. Therefore, when blacks incorporated religious themes into their blues, whether in jest or in earnest, the perceptions and sentiments that inspired the songs were entirely their own. Many blues artists sang clever lines about the unscrupulous deacon, the underhanded preacher, analogies between sex and salvation, and what they perceived as the dubious role of God. The tone of their singing was typically one of reflection and analysis, often tinged with spite.[3]

By the 1930s barriers between black and white audiences were beginning to give way beneath the force of records, radio, and the pursuit of profit. Black singers of popular music were less inclined to sing the blues and more likely, instead, to perform lighthearted music and songs with cross-cultural appeal, not for catharsis or social commentary, but for entertainment. As whites participated more and more in the production and consumption of music by blacks, comedy became the overwhelming context for popular songs that referenced or incorporated black folk religion. The black deacon and preacher were no longer simply topics in blues conversation; they became, instead, the subjects of burlesque mockery, distorted characterizations of black folk religion with an exaggerated emphasis on ignorance, hypocrisy, sexual misconduct, and greed. These caricatures of black religion in popular music reflected long-standing, racially carved misperceptions about blacks and their spirituality.

Negative perceptions about black folk religion are rooted in the way whites appraised black worship during the slave era. To a large degree, black slaves retained their West-African belief in the ritual of spirit possession. The physical exuberance associated with it was a valued and necessary part of the religious experience. Slave Christians thus favored spontaneity and spirit unction over the sobriety and structure found in white church settings. Unfamiliar with the West-African worldview that informed the slaves' style of expression, whites viewed black worship as wild, chaotic, and animalistic. After slavery, the membership in the black denominations that retained these folk elements to the highest degree tended to consist of the poorest and least educated blacks, while black denominations modeled after white churches consisted of blacks who were comparatively better off. Writing in 1892, white scholar H.K. Carroll summarized some of the most widespread beliefs about blacks and their religion:

> In his native condition . . . the Negro's religion generally is
> of a low and degraded type. . . . He pays divine honors to

his ugly, unshapely fetish; he resorts to cruel rites to
overcome malignant influences. . . . That the native African
passes quickly and easily from his heathen rites to those of
Islam and Christianity is a matter of common knowledge;
but that a poor, ignorant, superstitious slave boy should in
the course of a few years become an educated, dignified,
respected prelate of the Church of England shows that the
native African is not only capable of being educated and
Christianized, but of being polished in mind, manner, and
faith.[4]

Despite their belief that it was possible to "properly" convert blacks,
whites generally held a dim view of black religion and assumed the
Negro's morality to be intrinsically warped. Carroll continues:

The common idea respecting the Negro's religion is that it
is a crude and superficial form of Christianity and exercises
but little moral influence upon his life. He is religious,
intensely religious, many insist, but he is not moral. Faith
in a system which embraces and enforces the Ten Commandments and requires purity of life does not seem to him
inconsistent with the constant violation of one or more of
these commandments and with a notoriously impure career.
Caught in wrong acts and publicly exposed, he feels no
hesitancy in continuing his church duties and perceives no
incongruity between his profession and his guilty life.
Moreover, he is superstitious, still entertaining some of the
cruel notions of African savagery concerning witches and
evil possessions and using strange ceremonies to ward off
bad spirits. There may be voudou doctors among them and
peculiar exercises for the casting out of witches; no doubt,
many of them have ideas impossible to cultivated Christians. It would be strange if it were not so.[5]

Whites believed, furthermore, that the intensity and spontaneity
of black worship were peculiar maladies in need of correction, and
they applauded black clergymen who worked to suppress such be-

havior. In particular, Carroll praised the efforts of Bishop D.A. Payne, a black minister who was appalled by these folk worship practices. In his "Recollections of Seventy Years," Payne wrote about his own attempts to reform the way that blacks worshipped:

> In 1878 I attended a "bush-meeting," where I went to please the pastor whose circuit I was visiting. After the sermon they formed a ring, and with coats off sang, clapped their hands, and stamped their feet in a most ridiculous and heathenish way. I requested the pastor to go and stop their dancing. At his request, they stopped their dancing and clapping of hands, but remained singing and rocking their bodies to and fro. This they did for about fifteen minutes. I then went, and taking their leader by the arm requested him to desist and to sit down and sing in a rational manner. I told him also that it was a heathenish way to worship, and disgraceful to themselves, the race, and the Christian name. In that instance, they broke up their ring, but would not sit down, and walked sullenly away. After the sermon in the afternoon, having another opportunity of speaking alone to this young leader of the singing and clapping ring, he said, "Sinners won't get converted unless there is a ring." Said I, "you might sing till you fell down dead, and you would fail to convert a single sinner because nothing but the Spirit of God and the Word of God can convert sinners." He replied, "The Spirit of God works upon the people in different ways. At camp-meetings, there must be a ring here, a ring there, a ring over yonder, or sinners will not get converted." . . . These "bands" I have had to encounter in many places. . . . In some cases, all that I could do was to teach and preach the right, fit, and proper way of serving God.[6]

The Great Migration of blacks from South to North during World War I and the resulting emergence of a multitude of urban storefront churches between the 1910s and 1930s furthered the negative reputation of Southern-born, black folk worship. During this period, the established, mainline black churches in the North became over-crowded with the influx of newcomers from the South. In addition, many Southerners felt these churches to be too large, formal, and impersonal to meet their spiritual needs. Preferring, instead, the inti-macy and familiarity of smaller congregations made up of others like themselves, many established their own churches in storefronts, houses, and other improvised spaces where they could be free to sing, shout, clap, emote, and praise in the manner to which they were most accustomed. A historical look at the black church in Chicago yields a good example of just how common urban storefront churches were in the early decades of the twentieth century. In 1928, for example, 66 percent of Chicago's black Baptist churches and 86 percent of its Holiness/Pentecostal churches met in storefronts and houses, most of which were on the more economically depressed part of the city's South Side. These churches, which averaged about thirty members,

Physical expression is an important part of this worship service. Notice the man dancing, front, just left of center. (Photo courtesy of the Curtis Humphrey Photograph Collection, Texas African American Photography Archive, Documentary Arts, Inc., Dallas, Texas)

were the social and spiritual haven for those who found the older, established churches to be an ill fit.[7]

Because of their independence from mainline denominations, their uneducated clergy, and their position on the lowest rung of the socio-economic ladder, storefront churches and the groups to which they catered were objects of ridicule by blacks and whites alike. Black clergy of mainstream denominations considered them an embarrassment and a hindrance to racial progress. Although many Southern Baptist and Holiness/Pentecostal groups left the storefront to establish permanent and thriving congregations, they retained not only their charismatic worship style but also the stigma of their peculiarity and their humble beginnings. To those outside of these traditions, such enthusiastic worship was not only bizarre but was actually humorous and fit to be the butt of many a joke, not unlike the jokes found in the minstrel tradition.

Minstrelsy provides a highly picturesque account of the way whites perceived and interpreted blacks and their culture from the mid-nineteenth century until as recently as the late 1930s. William Mahar argues that minstrelsy had multiple meanings, poking fun not only at blacks, but at a variety of both marginal and aristocratic types in antebellum America. Although the blackened face typical of minstrelsy argues powerfully for the centrality of the African-American race to minstrel humor, it is true that minstrel portrayals of religion were often directed at the camp meeting and revivalist traditions which were distinguished, in part, by their racial integration. Influenced by the African-American example of emotional freedom, many whites were attracted to exuberant worship. There were several genres of religious parody in the minstrel tradition. One was the mock fundraising sermon, which ridiculed both black and white preachers who survived by collecting contributions from their followers. Another was the mock eulogy. Others poked fun directly at specific religious practices, like speaking in tongues or the speech-song style of the black preacher. Still other parodies questioned the moral integrity of fundamentalist and revivalist preachers. In virtually every case, religious styles associated with the low and marginal classes were the core of the joke. Mahar states that "blackface entertainers were well aware of the differences in behaviors and communal ritual practices among various black and white religious groups. Religion and religious issues appeared often in minstrelsy both as objects of ridicule and as subjects for quotation in a variety of verbal or musical parodies." Mahar includes the following quotation from "Trip to a Nigga Meeting" as an example of a minstrel script which "calls attention to the sheer emotional and physical power unleashed by the African-American preacher's sermons."[8]

> When I got to de meeting house,
> Dey say you better go,
> Kase you come to raise de debil here,
> and jump Jim Crow
> So I creep though de window;
> And sat myself a down,
> Broder Clem gub de text—
> Den dey hand de plate around
> In de ninty-lebenth chapter
> Ob de new Almanack
> Dar it tell you all about dare,
> De white man and de brack
> He says dat Cane was de fuss man,
> Julycome Cesar was de toder
> Dey put Adam on de treden mill,
> Kase he kill him broder
> And den dat Mr. Samson,
> was de man who build de Ark
> Mr. Jonas was de fisherman,
> Who swallowed down de shark.

Minstrelsy utilized religious caricature because religion was one of the most powerful indicators of racial and class differentiation. For audiences of minstrel shows, pieces like "Trip to a Nigga Meeting" confirmed the huge cultural gap between themselves and blacks.

In order to have theatrical careers, many blacks assumed the denigrating antics of minstrelsy, portraying what whites considered the most amusing behaviors and characteristics of blacks and their culture. That whites found black religion amusing is further shown by

These images suggest the degree to which late nineteenth and early twentieth-century Americans valued minstrel entertainment. (Photos courtesy of the Center for Popular Music, Murfreesboro, Tennessee)

Bert Williams's performances of the religious farce "Oh Death, Where Is Thy Sting?" recorded in 1918, and the Elder Eatmore Sermons, one called "Generosity," the other "Throwing Stones," both recorded in 1919. A master minstrel, Williams, who was black, had perfected the broken grammar and shiftless mannerisms to a degree that won him thunderous applause from white audiences from the 1910s through the 1930s. He uses them expertly in the Elder Eatmore sermons, in which he plays the greedy, ignorant Elder Eatmore who mispronounces and bungles scripture for personal gain. The Elder Eatmore caricature is even embellished with fictitious congregational singing by parishioners who are presumably oblivious to the Elder's ineptness and as ignorant as he is. This particular parody is aimed directly at black Holiness/Pentecostal groups, as these groups typically address their ministers with the title *Elder* as opposed to *Reverend,* the latter being more typical in Baptist churches. In "Oh Death, Where Is Thy Sting?" Williams casts a shadow on black morality and mocks the traditional African-American belief in the afterlife by singing, "If hell is full of women, whiskey, and dice, then death, where is thy sting?" Although Williams played to white audiences, many blacks shared the sentiments about folk religion implicit in the Elder Eatmore parodies. Southern blacks migrating northward by the thousands in the late 1910s constituted an underclass distinguished by their appearance, their dialect, and their social and religious customs. Black Northerners often treated the newcomers with condescension. Although established, mainline black churches made efforts to accommodate folk worship, these efforts, at least early on, were cautious and guarded at best. Michael Harris writes about the clash of Northern and Southern black religious cultures in Chicago:

> When migrants first arrived, old-line ministers seem to
> have adopted the attitude that emotionalism, if tempered,
> would be tolerated. Around 1915, Elijah J. Fisher, pastor of
> Olivet Baptist Church, "believed in enthusiastic religion
> but did not countenance a church in demoniac pandemo-
> nium." By the end of the 1920s Junius C. Austin, pastor of
> Pilgrim Baptist Church, believed his success hinged on
> keeping the congregation "dignified" but giving them

"what they wanted in the pulpit." Thus, he appears to have utilized the techniques of folk preaching, while at the same time allowing only the response he thought appropriate to the urban church.[9]

Folk worship and its adherents were thus regarded as a threat to the dignified image to which the Northern, urban church aspired.

By the 1930s, Bert Williams's brand of minstrelsy was on the decline and other forms of popular entertainment—most notably, jazz and popular song—had become avenues for black musical artists. In some popular tunes from this era that parody revivalist religion, it is difficult to say conclusively that the humor is directed specifically at African Americans since many lower-class whites embraced Pentecostal and revivalist traditions and incorporated spontaneity and visible enthusiasm into their worship. Such practices, however, were generally believed to have been clearly influenced by blacks, and mainstream whites often characterized their "excesses" as consistent with "nigger behavior." Another element that black and white revivalist traditions had in common was the Evangelical heritage emphasizing both hatred of sin and the conversion of sinners. The sense of moral superiority afforded by this point of view was perhaps in lieu of economic, educational, and social opportunities. Nonetheless, popular songwriters ridiculed what they perceived as the inherent dogmatism and moral arrogance of these traditions.

"Sing, You Sinners!" recorded in 1930 by the Harlem Hot Chocolates, is an excellent example of such a parody. The group includes Duke Ellington, several of Ellington's musicians, and Ellington's white publisher, Irving Mills, who is the vocalist on the recording:

"Sing, You Sinners!" by the Harlem Hot Chocolates

You sinners, drop everything
and let that harmony ring
up to heaven and sing
Sing you sinners!
Just wave your arms all about
and let the law hear you shout
all that music right out

White evangelicals holding a revival in the woods, circa 1890. (Photo courtesy of the Center for Popular Music, Murfreesboro, Tennessee)

Sing you sinners!
Whenever there's music, the Devil kicks
He don't allow music by the river Styx
You're wicked and you're depraved
and you all misbehave
If you wanna be saved,
Just sing, you sinners!

The tune, which features a lengthy instrumental introduction before Mills sings, pokes fun at the common view of sin among many folk religious traditions. A satire on this revivalist perspective, the song encourages sinners not to repent but to sing. Lines like "Just wave your arms all about," "let the law hear you shout," and "if you wanna be saved, Just sing" clearly reference the emphasis on conversion in the revivalist perspective. The admonitions are, of course, as tongue-in-cheek as is LaVern Baker's "testimony" in "Saved." The real message here is for sinners to revel in their decadence. The parody not only ridicules a religious perspective but also underscores a huge class distinction between cultured, aristocratic blacks like Duke Ellington and black immigrants from the South.

Although Ellington's role in "Sing, You Sinners!" was significant, evidence suggests that the idea for this recording may have come from Mills. Mills was a songwriter, music publisher, and recording artist who had amassed considerable clout in the music business by 1930. He became Ellington's manager in 1923 and was said to have personally engineered and supervised Ellington's success in the recording industry, even to the extent of deciding which recordings Ellington would or would not release.[10]

In the late 1920s and 1930s, at least six different versions of a highly popular quartet piece, "Do You Call That Religion?" were recorded. Renditions of this sacred piece were released by the Birmingham Jubilee Singers (1926), the Kentucky Jubilee Four and the Utica Institute Jubilee Singers (both in 1927), Bryant's Jubilee Quartet (1928), the Hall Negro Quartet (1936) and the Spartanburg Famous Four (also in 1936). This piece, which rebukes Christians for practicing non-Christian behavior, was so popular that it may have been the basis for Duke Ellington's "Is That Religion?" recorded in 1931 while Ellington was still under the management of Irving Mills. Unlike what seems to be its sacred counterpart, "Is That Religion?" is pure comedy. The lyrics are sung by a fictitious "preacher" who uses a highly theatrical, burlesque singing style. With Ellington's big band as accompaniment, the vocalist rebukes the church "sisters" who "just strut the aisle / all dressed to kill with style." The vocalist continues: "One thing I do despise / you catch my deacon's eyes / and that's where the weakness lies / Is that religion?" Ellington's "Is

That Religion?" reinforces the stereotype of the black church as a place not of devotion but of unbridled sexuality. This theme surfaces time and again in popular songs recorded in the years following. Of particular interest is a rendition of "Is That Religion?" recorded by Mildred Bailey in 1933. Bailey, who is considered by many to be the first successful white jazz singer, retains most of the elements of Ellington's 1931 version of the tune. However, she adds the lines "Ain't it a shame to trifle on Sunday when you got Monday, Tuesday, Wednesday, Thursday, Friday, and Saturday too!" Although she makes a nebulous attempt at black dialect, the ethnic direction of the humor is as clear in her recording as it is in Ellington's.

In the same year that she recorded "Is That Religion?" Mildred Bailey released another satire on black folk worship, "Shoutin' in the Amen Corner." As is frequently the case, the lyrics are sung from the perspective of the fictitious, irate black preacher who rebukes his flock for moral delinquency. In a race/gender twist that is comical in itself, Bailey sings lines like "If your name ain't on that roll / all that noise won't save your soul!" and "I can't hear my own self preachin' / for your shoutin' and your screechin'!" As a white woman doing a caricature of a black preacher, Bailey's satire is multidimensional, attacking black male leadership, folk worship practice, and black morality all at once.

Although minstrelsy declined in the 1930s, it was far from dead. Picking up where Elder Eatmore had left off, black entertainers continued to use minstrel antics into the 1940s and 1950s to parody and satirize black folk religion. The continued popularity of these caricatures in secular music after 1930 may well have been in reaction to a new wave of South-to-North black migration from 1932 to 1940. During these years, thousands of Southern blacks sought jobs in Northern industrial centers—again, bringing with them their native religious customs. A recurring stereotype in these satirical songs is that of the black deacon. Invariably characterized as a womanizing, dice-throwing, closet drunk, the deacon stereotype symbolizes the perception that black spiritual leaders are morally depraved and black religion is, thus, essentially a joke.

Several black secular performers recorded "deacon" caricature tunes in the 1940s and 1950s. Louis Jordan, best known for his colorful, witty lyrics, recorded such a tune in 1943. His appetite for cross-over success was encouraged by his white manager, Berle Adams, who urged Jordan to incorporate comedy into his act. Adams states, "Louis wanted to be thought of primarily as a fine musician. He knew all the show tunes and could play them well, but I said to him, 'Look, you're never going to be a Johnny Hodges or a Willie Smith—be a showman.' I was always on his tail to be a comic. I could see he excelled at that. So one day, he did a Deacon Jones thing he'd learnt way back, he put on a stove-pipe hat and he was wonderful."[11]

First in 1943 and at least twice more in the years to follow, Jordan released recordings of "Deacon Jones" and, as did Adams, white audiences loved the minstrel flavor of the performance, which underscored and reinforced their misguided beliefs about black folk religion. Like many of Jordan's tunes, "Deacon Jones" is a humorous, jump blues piece in which he sings to the "flock" about the expert womanizer, Deacon Jones. Lines like, "Now, when a sister's feelin' blue, who consoles her in her pew" and "When your gal is leavin' you, tell me who she's goin' to" are answered by the refrain, "Lawdy Lawd, Hallelujah, Deacon Jones!"

In 1946, Lucky Millinder recorded "Fare Thee Well, Deacon Jones." Singing in dialect to the accompaniment of his band, Millinder tells the story of the untimely "death" of Deacon Jones:

Gather 'roun' me chillun while I tell the news
I hate to tell about it cause I gets the blues
No one knows about it but my wife
But you can bet she saw the Deacon when he lost his life

The implication, of course, is that the Deacon was having an affair with the narrator's wife. The song continues with the story of the Deacon's fall to his "death" in the well: "He was down there drinkin' juice / when the bucket, it broke loose." The words "well" and "juice" are both double entendres, meaning either sex or liquor. The narrator continues, "He fell in at around nine, and his dice jumped in behind." In the end, however, the Deacon is not dead after all: "I wouldda been dead but the well was dry." Millinder's tune contains all of the classic elements of the deacon caricature.

In 1949, the Orioles recorded another tune entitled "Deacon Jones" which actually has more in common with Lucky Millinder's "Fare Thee Well, Deacon Jones" than with Jordan's tune of the same title. The tune tells of Deacon Jones's funeral: "Well, it was early Monday mornin', the church was very bare / the roof was really leakin', and the rain was everywhere / the whole congregation stayed at home / so poor Deacon Jones was left alone." A lone woman at the Deacon's funeral proclaims, "he was my ol' man for years, but he sho' could shift his gears." As in Millinder's tune, the Deacon isn't dead after all. He begins to rise from the coffin "with bloodshot eyes" to proclaim "I'm the greatest deacon the world has ever seen / you all hate Deacon Jones 'cause all my chicks are in their teens!" In addition to the drunkard and womanizer stereotypes, this version of "Deacon Jones" contains a direct reference to social class. The "leaky roof" in the story is imagery suggestive of the black underclass—people who didn't gather to worship in stained glass buildings but in storefronts and other impoverished places.

In the early 1950s, the legacy of caricature continued. In 1951, Little Esther Phillips recorded "The Deacon Moves In." With an accompaniment provided by the Dominoes, "The Deacon Moves In" is a conversation between the sex-starved Deacon and Sister Pigeon. The song begins with Sister Pigeon: "Look out there Deacon / Do you really think I'm gonna weaken?" He replies: "Well now, Sister Pigeon / If you really want that true religion / You betta do what I say and see this thing my way." After the Deacon has successfully seduced Sister Pigeon, she sings "Got that true religion. . . . Lay down that gin and kiss me once again!"

In 1953 Wynonie Harris recorded "The Deacon Don't Like It," in which he sings of the "evils" of switching from whiskey to moonshine, and his admonition is punctuated with the refrain, "And the Deacon don't like it!" He points to the stereotype of the Deacon as womanizer near the end: "Now some of you sisters in this congregation / Sing in the choir and the usher board too / You used to wear your dresses so short, people had to talk / Now you wearin' em so long, you can hardly walk / And the Deacon don't like it!"

Although the popularity of these deacon caricature tunes may be related to racist attitudes of whites and condescending attitudes of some blacks, the texts of these recordings should not be considered apart from the larger context of African-American folklore. Other factors notwithstanding, African Americans have long nurtured a rich tradition of jokelore in which self-directed humor is considered quite entertaining. This humor includes a wealthy repertoire of self-defaming "inside jokes" about black church life in which the deacon is the central character. These recordings might thus be considered the musical versions of any number of African-American folktales about religion that poke fun at black clergymen. Transmitted orally, a single tale may exist in more than one version. Its essential plot and punchline, however, tend to remain intact.

From among this vast body of jokelore, I cite just a couple of folktales that are thematically similar to the deacon caricature tunes included in this study. With slight paraphrasing, the stories are presented here the way they are conveyed in Daryl Cumber Dance's *Shuckin' and Jivin': Folklore from Contemporary Black Americans* (1978).

Deacon Brown is Dead!

The Negro Deacon who had the largest sex organ in town had a habit of making all of the Sisters happy in the church. And at church time, they would all go up and press his hand. The Minister had become sort of jealous of it. He didn't do anything. So he (the Deacon) died. And they couldn't do anything at all to get his sex organ in the casket with him. He died seemingly with a hard-on and they just couldn't get the thing to go down. So they had to cut it off and place it beside him—open of course. His last will said let his remains remain open. When the funeral was over, they carried the body on down to the grave and buried the body. But they forgot that they had left his penis in this little case they had for it. So the Minister said, "Well, I won't be that rotten. I'll take it on home and tomorrow I'll take it to the cemetery to be placed in the Deacon's grave. So he took it home. His wife later came to serve the Minister his tea when she turned and saw the case containing the Deacon's penis. She broke down and cried, "Deacon Brown is dead!!"[12]

Shall We Gather at the River

> One Sunday the Preacher got up in the pulpit and he started
> to preachin'. He say, "For my part, you can take all the
> whiskey and throw it in the river." An old Deacon in the
> front say, "Amen!" He say, "For my part, you can take all
> the wine and throw it in the river." The Deacon said,
> "Amen!" again. He said, "For my part, you can take all of
> the alcohol and throw it in the river!" The Deacon say,
> "Amen!" So he ended his sermon. The Deacon jumped up.
> He say, "Let us sing page 392, 'Shall We Gather at the
> River.'"[13]

The textual link between folktales like these and deacon caricature
tunes is undeniable.

The popularity of deacon caricature tunes suggests the potency
of negative stereotypes about black religious leadership. Most black
artists who recorded such tunes had personal roots in the black Baptist and Pentecostal traditions, although these ties generally dissolved
as the artists pursued secular careers. An exception is Rosetta Tharpe,
who recorded secular sides while maintaining a lifelong connection
to the Church of God in Christ.

Tharpe was a gospel music prodigy who sang and played the
guitar to assist her mother, a Pentecostal traveling evangelist. At
around twenty years of age, Tharpe moved to New York and in 1938
secured a contract with Decca records. The producers at Decca, however, wanted Tharpe's music to have wider appeal than the churchgoing black community. Consequently, they revised her style by
replacing sacred titles with secular ones and by using Lucky
Millinder's orchestra along with her own guitar accompaniment.
Decca thus launched Tharpe into the record-buying mainstream, and
she became an instant celebrity.

In 1938, and again in 1943, she recorded a rendition of Thomas
Dorsey's gospel tune "Hide Me in Thy Bosom" under the title "Rock
Me." The side begins with a brief introduction featuring Tharpe's
virtuosic feats on the guitar, accompanied by Lucky Millinder's or-

Sister Rosetta Tharpe (Photo courtesy of the Center for Popular Music, Murfreesboro, Tennessee)

chestra. From beginning to end, the song teeters on the boundary separating sacred meaning from secular farce. The jazzy saxophone licks in the orchestra (in the 1940s, such licks were avowedly profane) further cloud Tharpe's meaning, making it impossible to conclude whether the song is a prayer to God for comfort or a coded appeal to a Don Juan deacon for the kind of "religion" that Sister Pigeon achieves in "The Deacon Moves In." When Tharpe sings the line beginning with the words, "Rock me," she uses a seductive throatiness, further tipping the balance in favor of secular farce. Tharpe was a deeply religious and perhaps somewhat naive Pentecostal woman, and she may well have imagined herself singing to God in this tune. But consumers heard satire and caricature in "Rock Me," not prayer and devotion.

When Tharpe employed the secular trappings, she effectively excommunicated herself from her beloved Church of God in Christ. Although she continued to attend services after her Decca release, hers was a losing battle for the church's acceptance, as they now viewed her as a backslider. Even when she performed in gospel settings later in her life, Tharpe's show-business image overshadowed her church roots. Her religious image had gone from authentic to satirical. The producers at Decca billed her as Sister Rosetta Tharpe, and they knowingly capitalized on the humorous irony of a "Sister" Tharpe singing "Rock Me," the double entendre hardly subtle.

In another of Tharpe's releases, "Strange Things Happening Everyday" (1944), Tharpe performs what amounts to a response to the Sanctified church's criticism of her performance style. The song opens with the line, "Oh we hear church people say they are in the 'Holy Way.'" The lyrics that follow condemn their self-righteous behavior and the refrain, "There are strange things happening everyday," punctuates the unfolding of the text. Tharpe's backup on this song consists of the trio of instrumentalists who double as the vocal "congregation" in this call-and-response tune. Horace Boyer writes: "Surprising to some, Tharpe did not choose one of the established gospel quartets such as the Soul Stirrers or the Dixie Hummingbirds to serve as the congregation to her preaching. Instead, she used the trio accompanying her, which sang in voices suggestive of cynicism, satire, and levity. In the final analysis, it was a perfect mixing, because 'Strange Things Happening Everyday' was on the borderline between sacred music and secular music."[14] For the church, the satire created by the Pentecostal "Sister" against the secular backdrop was inherently blasphemous. The tension between her secular popularity and her church heritage was evident throughout her life.

By the 1930s, black music, as an ethnic category, was accepted and appreciated by the mainstream. The gamut of black musical styles, however, also included those artists who modeled their songs and their performances according to the standards of white popular music. Black vocal groups like the Mills Brothers and the Ink Spots, for example, became known for their airtight harmonies, their vocal precision, and their lighthearted, middle-of-the-road repertoire. Because of their largely white appeal, such groups are frequently omitted from discussions about mid-century black popular music. But they constitute an important facet of black music history, symbolizing in a very graphic way the nexus between white aesthetics and black aspiration.

The Ink Spots, in particular, were highly popular with whites and by the mid-1940s had become one of the most widely known secular quartets in existence. Although the group originated in 1934 in Indiana, personnel changes and spin-off groups in the 1950s altered the original makeup of the Ink Spots. These spin-off groups, seeking to emulate the style and success of the original group, continued some of the minstrel antics that had helped to popularize the quartet in the 1930s and 1940s. One notable example is a recording of "When the Saints Go Marching In," popularized in the 1930s as a jazz standard by Louis Armstrong. The performance in question was done on the Pirouette label during a live session in Las Vegas. Although little is known about the Pirouette label and no date is given on the record jacket itself, scholars believe this recording to be one of a few lackluster releases by one of the spin-off Ink Spots groups in the 1950s.[15]

The tune begins in the usual way, but soon the singing quartet gives way to a short theatrical interlude as the band continues to play. One of the singers adopts a guttural preacher voice, and as he fashions a highly caricatured, nonsensical sermon, the other members of the quartet egg him on. "Hallelujah!!," "Amen!!" (in over-dramatized female falsettos), "Yes Brother!!" and "Preach It!!" punctuate the ramblings of the "preacher" until the quartet returns to singing. Its dubious origin notwithstanding, this rendition of "When the Saints Go Marching In" is reminiscent of minstrelsy.

Although minstrel antics were tolerated by blacks and applauded by whites in the 1930s and 1940s, they didn't sit so well with the black community by the 1950s. When Ivory "Deek" Watson performed with the late 1950s version of the Ink Spots, he retained what the *Chicago Daily Defender* called "Uncle Tom techniques" which offended the black community. Just as Watson and his antics were considered passé by midcentury, comedic treatments of black religion by blacks were becoming highly unpopular in an era during which the black church would play a crucial political and symbolic role in the struggle for civil rights.[16]

I have argued that religious caricature in black popular music reflects appraisals of black religion rooted in minstrelsy, the conflict between black Southern and Northern religious cultures, and the African-American tradition of religious jokelore. In addition to these factors, black religious caricature at midcentury may also reflect other social conditions. In an article on "Catholics of Color" in its November 1945 issue, *Ebony* magazine reported that "some 8 million Negroes claim no religious affiliation whatsoever." This number, considered in tandem with 1946 population statistics, suggests that in 1945 just over half of African Americans were unchurched. Therefore, in addition to expanded Northern churches and a proliferation of storefront churches, another effect of migration was the redefinition of church as a focal institution in African-American life. Black newcomers to the urban scene in the 1930s and 1940s found a variety of spiritual options competing for their allegiance. Along with traditional black Christianity, creative revisions of Christianity, black Messianic figures, charlatans, and frauds found easy prey in the transplanted Southerners desperate for a sense of belonging and connection. Finding a place in neither traditional churches nor in any of the new religious groups, many blacks simply dismissed organized religion altogether. The caricatures in black popular song may thus also reflect not just a reaction to the religious customs of a specified group but also a generalized disillusionment with traditional religion as a governing concept. For the blacks who did fall away, urban life in the

North would present an alternative to organized religion. In the 1930s, the first of the black radio announcers began to emerge, and, in the decades following, they became social heroes, addressing the black community from a forum where gospel and the blues and other sacred and secular phenomena mingled freely. With his elevated status in the community and ability to address and influence thousands of blacks across the airwaves, the black deejay—particularly in the late 1940s and afterward—stood in stark contrast to the black country preacher or deacon, whose influence was limited and whose life could easily become the target of scrutiny.[17]

By the time LaVern Baker recorded "Saved" in 1961, the black church had taken on a new political significance. North/South differences were supplanted by the important work of the Civil Rights Movement, a movement which could not afford satirical affronts on black male religious leadership and African-American folk culture from within its own ranks. The decline of deacon caricature tunes by the 1960s may be explained by the fact that many of the most commanding and influential figures in the Civil Rights Movement were black Baptist clergymen from the South. Frequently risking their lives to bring about positive change for African Americans, black deacons and preachers nullified the stereotypes of buffoonery and drunkenness in the parodies by Millinder, Jordan, and others so popular in earlier years. Furthermore, it was no longer popular to satirize the folkways of the grassroots blacks who gave steam to the Movement. As it became common for black churches in the South to host civil rights meetings, it became just as common for black churches to be bombed and burned throughout the 1960s. Against the backdrop of these serious conditions, black popular song replaced Elder Eatmore and Deacon Jones with new religious images more indicative of the times.

4

RETHINKING THE DEVIL'S MUSIC

Integration, Religion, and Crossing Over

The son of a minister, Sam Cooke developed his musical talent in the church. His position as lead singer with the Soul Stirrers was the gospel prerequisite for his graduation to the broader, more lucrative world of mainstream pop. The transition from gospel to secular music was a road paved at times with more guilt than gold, since die-hard church folk considered him a backslider. Davin Seay and Mary Neely describe the inner struggle of numerous black artists caught between the pull of the church and the lure of the secular world during the nascent years of rhythm and blues. They state that "the lives of men like Sam Cooke and Little Richard were marked by bondage to an overpowering, unending conflict. . . . It's useless to speculate on what such men might have accomplished had they not spent half of their lives rebelling against religious strictures and the other half trying guiltily to make amends."[1] Although Cooke's inner struggle typifies that of many gospel-born secular artists, it represents but one aspect of the many implications of crossing over from gospel to secular music during the 1950s. This phenomenon is a telling indicator of black religious, racial, and economic sensibilities at midcentury and should be viewed within the larger context of a black-American social and political evolution.

Sam Cooke was neither the first nor the last black artist to sever his church ties in pursuit of secular glory. His particular transition from the church to the world is significant, though, for at least two reasons. First, he was the first widely celebrated professional gospel singer to seek a secular career. Although numerous gospel artists had done so before him, none were nearly as famous as Sam Cooke. Second, the year of his transition—1956—points to a period during which black religious and racial sentiments lay at a pivotal crossroads. It was during this time that changes in American society brought about a rethinking of traditional black-American religious values. While much has been written about the pervasiveness of gospel stylings in black secular music, relatively little has been written about crossing over as an indicator of black America's shifting religious consciousness.

Powerful notions of good versus evil, of sanctity versus sin, and of God versus the Devil governed the religious perspective of blacks who viewed secular music as the forbidden fruit of youthful excess. From this perspective, music was either God's or the Devil's, with little to no gray area in between. Vocalist Cissy Houston voiced the experience of many black artists when she stated: "I had been brought up strict, to think that all of it, rock and all, was the Devil's music."[2] Beliefs about the Devil and his music are generations-old in the black-American psyche. Although the first Africans to arrive in the Colonies had no concept of a sacred/secular distinction in music or in any other aspect of life, black Americans incorporated this duality into their awareness as a result of exposure to Western culture. In addition, the nineteenth-century Evangelical and Holiness movements, which stressed pious living as evidence of religious conversion, further reinforced the distinction between sacred and secular in black-American thought. Many blacks found the Holiness and Evangelical movements particularly attractive since they offered avenues for moral superiority in an era when social, political, and economic power was unattainable. In order to achieve this behaviorial superiority, they maintained a clear conceptual separation between the things that were God's and those that were the Devil's.[3]

In the 1920s and 1930s, blues artists sang what churchgoing blacks invariably labeled "the Devil's music." Heard in brothels, juke joints, and other places beyond the church walls, these songs turned a spotlight on the pain and pleasure of human existence. Thoroughly raunchy at times, blues texts also contained many thoughtful analyses of religion, not to mention scathing critiques of church life. The abun-

dance of religious commentary in the blues suggests that these singers were deeply invested in spiritual matters, though standing on the
outer perimeter of the church looking in. Jon Michael Spencer states
that "while the 'quite religious' had the opportunity to express their
mythologies, theologies, and theodicies in their church music, the
'somewhat religious' expressed their cosmology and religious
ponderings in the blues." The black church was particularly offended
by bluesmen and women who sang both racy material and traditional
hymns. Looking to access the then more lucrative religious market,
many blues singers, including Robert Johnson, Charlie Patton, Blind
Lemon Jefferson, Son House, and Memphis Minnie, recorded religious material. For such digressions, Blind Lemon Jefferson recorded
as "Deacon L.J. Bates" and Memphis Minnie became "Gospel
Minnie." In the eyes of the church, this shameless oscillation between God and the Devil may have been more offensive than the
content of any *jellyroll* or *peach orchard* tune.[4]

Beliefs about the Devil's music also extended to certain types of
instrumentation. In his autobiography, *Father of the Blues,* W.C.
Handy writes about his parents' reaction to his purchase of a new
guitar: "'A box,' he gasped while my mother stood frozen. 'A guitar!
One of the Devil's playthings. . . . Whatever possessed you to bring a
sinful thing like that into our Christian home?' . . . Brought up to
regard guitars and other stringed instruments as devices of Satan, he
could scarcely believe that a son of his could have the audacity to
bring one of them into his house."[5]

Many blacks, particularly in the South, entertained various beliefs about the Devil as the source of otherwise unexplainable musical talent. The ritual selling of one's soul to the Devil in exchange for
musical skill was well known in the South, and a New Orleans con-
jurer described the procedure as follows:

If you want to make a contact with the Devil, first trim
your finger nails as close as you possibly can. Take a black
cat bone and a guitar and go to a lonely fork in the roads at
midnight. Sit down there and play your best piece, thinking
of and wishing for the Devil all the while. By and by you
will hear music, dim at first but growing louder and louder

as the musician approaches nearer. Do not look around; just
keep on playing your guitar. The unseen musician will
finally sit down by you and play in unison with you. After a
time you will feel something tugging at your instrument.
Do not try to hold it. Let the Devil take it and keep thump-
ing along with your fingers as if you still had a guitar in
your hands. Then the Devil will hand you his instrument to
play and will accompany you on yours. After doing this for
a time he will seize your fingers and trim the nails until
they bleed, finally taking his guitar back and returning your
own. Keep on playing; don't look around. His music will
become fainter and fainter as he moves away. When all is
quiet you may go home.[6]

Virtuosic blues artist Robert Johnson was said to have made such a
pact with the Devil in exchange for his remarkable musical abilities.
Indeed, many of Johnson's blues, such as "Hellhound on My Trail"
and "Me and the Devil Blues," bespeak visions of an unescapable
evil. It is said that Johnson's death by poisoning in 1938, supposedly
at the hand of a jealous husband, was the Devil coming to claim
Johnson's bartered soul.[7] Although Johnson's story is perhaps the
most oft-repeated version of the legend, he was one of several secular artists believed to have gotten their talents through dealings with
the Devil. Bluesman Johnny Shines of Memphis would later say of
Chester Burnett, better known as Howlin' Wolf, that "a guy who played
like [that], he'd sold his soul to the Devil."[8]

By the 1940s, the Devil's music had evolved into rhythm and
blues, and between the late 1940s and the 1960s, virtually all noteworthy black secular artists hailed from the pews, quartets, and choirs
of the black church. Louis Jordan attended services with his aunt,
who was the church pianist, long before he joined Chick Webb's band.
Before she changed her name to Dinah Washington, Ruth Lee Jones
had come of age in the Sanctified church and sang gospel with the
Sallie Martin Singers. Before she became "Miss Rhythm," Ruth
Brown "got happy" at the Methodist church where her father was a
minister. The Royal Sons marked their shift to secular music by changing their name to the Five Royales, and the Gospel Starlighters be-

came James Brown and the Famous Flames upon their switch to
rhythm and blues. Johnny Ace, the son of a minister, sang and played
hymns on the family piano before his secular career. Clyde McPhatter,
also the son of a minister, soloed as a boy soprano in the Baptist
church before his fame in the secular arena.[9]

There is much evidence to counter Brian Ward's assertion that
the black church does not seem to have had a great influence on the
development of northern rhythm and blues. Several of the most important northern doo-wop groups were either born of church roots or
were church-affiliated at the time of their inceptions. Billy Ward was
a gospel coach in Harlem before he formed the Dominoes. James
"Pookie" Hudson of the Spaniels (formed in Gary, Indiana, in the
early 1950s) was singing in gospel choirs when he met Billy Shelton
and Calvin Fossett, two of the group's original members. Formed in
1951 in Philadelphia, the Silhouettes' original members were named
the Gospel Tornadoes and performed in the local church circuit. Both
Frankie Lymon and the Teenagers and Lewis Lymon and the Teen
Chords had church music roots that could be traced to the Lymon
patriarch, Frankie Lymon Sr. The elder Lymon, who had a gospel
group called the Harlemaires, was the primary musical influence upon
his two sons. Boston's G-Clefs began singing in the parish choir of
their Catholic church. And Zola Taylor of the Platters cites her own
church roots when she recalls being scolded by her mother for "hittin'
boogie-woogie on the piano on a Sunday when I was supposed to be
playing church music."[10]

The literature—both scholarly and popular—is replete with accounts of rhythm-and-blues artists whose training in musicianship,
stage presence, and audience interaction come directly from the black
church. These accounts, far too numerous to rehearse here, seem to
suggest that since the 1940s a firsthand, formative experience with
music in the black church has been a virtual prerequisite for success
in the world of rhythm and blues.

This prerequisite also applied to nonblacks who ventured into
rhythm and blues. The son of Greek immigrant parents, Johnny Otis
grew up in a predominantly black neighborhood in Berkeley, California. George Lipsitz writes: "He remembers that his first fascination with black culture came from accompanying some of his black

playmates to church. The churches provided Graham crackers and chocolate milk for children. . . . But Otis soon realized that it was more than the Graham crackers and chocolate milk; that the sounds of the gospel choirs, the enthusiasm of the congregations, and the intellectual and moral power of the preachers spoke to him in profound ways."[11] This experience not only helped to fuel Otis's musical prowess, but gave him unique credentials to maneuver successfully, as a white man, in a world that was predominantly black. In fact, it was Johnny Otis who recruited Willie Mae Thornton, a minister's daughter, and Little Esther Phillips, a member of the Sanctified church, to the world of rhythm and blues.

There are several ways that the black church played a vital role in the shaping of rhythm-and-blues artistry. The northward migration of blacks, first in the 1910s and 1920s, and later during the World War II era, weakened the traditional influence of the black church on African-American life. Nevertheless, the church remained the most important and most easily accessible forum for cultural and creative expression. Particularly in the folk denominations, even the least educated, least articulate, least talented blacks found in the church a safe, nurturing environment where encouragement was guaranteed and feedback was immediate. In such a community, spirit possession outranked precision. Missed notes or forgotten lyrics were easily forgiven if a singer could otherwise effectively move and enliven the congregation. Another factor is that age discrimination was, and continues to be, nonexistent in the black church. In denominations which value spontaneity, even the youngest of children participate in the church's musical activities, where they learn gospel performance through listening, imitation, and improvisation. Therefore, by the time such a child is a teenager, he or she is already well-versed in the types of musicianship skills that transfer easily into the arena of secular performance. The black church also provided young artists with their first exposure to performance for pay, usually in the form of freewill offerings. The prospect of earning money, not to mention respect and prestige in the community, served as powerful incentive for young gospel artists to develop their talents to the highest possible degree.

By the 1950s, much about the performance of God's music had become secularized. Although gospel singers frequently received freewill offerings from appreciative congregations, artists had already embraced the notion of charging admission for gospel performances as early as 1936. It was during this year that Thomas Dorsey reputedly became the first to charge admission to a singing competition between gospel divas Roberta Martin and Sallie Martin.[12] This entrepreneurial spirit was one of the catalysts that pushed gospel music beyond the confines of the church. In the 1930s, gospel artists could be heard at community events, in theaters, in auditoriums, and on radio. The development of black-oriented radio programming in the late 1940s and 1950s brought an increased demand for recorded black gospel, which independent labels including Apollo, Savoy, Specialty, and Vee Jay provided. Horace Boyer describes how the Clara Ward Singers, gospel music's most famous female group of the 1950s, exemplified star quality and secular flare:

> The Ward Singers set the standard for all female gospel groups. They led the way in vocal arrangements, uniforms, dress (The Ward Singers eventually sang in sequined gowns), and mode of travel (Cadillacs with trailers.) They were the first gospel group to wear exaggerated coiffured wigs at a time when women were ridiculed for wearing "false" hair. Mrs. Ward jealously protected her singers, demanded grand fees for performances, juggled programming so that the Ward Singers would appear in the most lucrative places on the program, and even resorted to taking up special collections when she felt they had been underpaid.[13]

Audience reaction to gospel artists during this period also bore the stamp of carnality. Writing about the popularity of male gospel quartet performances in the 1940s and 1950s, Kip Lornell states that "the crowds' outward reactions were hardly alien to those of fans of the era's best-known black pop singers—Louis Jordan, Hank Ballard, Dinah Washington. . . . This level of popularity brought out a type of adulation that sometimes bordered on the sexual."[14]

This blurring of boundaries between God and the Devil at midcentury shows how the sacred/secular dichotomy in black thought, while pronounced, is rather convoluted and problematic. In actual practice, blacks have always obscured the boundaries between sacred and secular, inserting fragments of hymns in their blues and using pop tunes as accompaniment for religious texts. In the 1950s, this fusion between the holy and the profane was documented on millions of records that were widely accessible to millions of eager consumers. If this type of stylistic cross-fertilization is the work of the Devil, then he (or she) is perhaps more accurately characterized as the African trickster god *Legba* rather than as the decidedly sinister figure of Western thought. In the Yoruba belief system, Legba serves seemingly contradictory functions in human affairs. Describing the duplicity of Legba and its relationship to the blues, Spencer writes that this deity "is both malevolent and benevolent, disruptive and reconciliatory, profane and sacred, and yet the predominant attitude toward him is affection rather than fear."[15] The irony, of course, was that by the 1950s, blacks who were most successful at "the Devil's music" were able to access many of the very opportunities for which ordinary blacks had struggled and prayed throughout their history in America.

It was during the late 1940s and 1950s that many of the most celebrated black artists discovered that they could trade in their choir robes for secular music and the material elements of the American dream. However, for too many of these "prodigal son" rhythm-and-blues artists, the dream ended in a nightmare. Johnny Ace committed suicide in a mindless game of Russian roulette on Christmas Eve, 1954. Jesse Belvin died in a car accident in 1960. Dinah Washington died of an overdose of sleeping pills in 1963. Sam Cooke died of a gunshot wound in 1964, and Otis Redding in a plane crash three years later in 1967. Clyde McPhatter died an alcoholic in 1972, Donny Hathaway fell to his death from the fifteenth floor of a hotel in 1979, and Marvin Gaye was shot to death by his father in 1984. The tragic ends of these artists, all of whom were once either amateur or professional gospel singers, tend to conjure up images of the Robert Johnson legend. In exchange for their stardom, some would say, the Devil had come to collect his due.

This point of view is expressed clearly in the reaction of Leslie Alexander to the death of her son, Johnny Ace. A staunch church member who had opposed her son's involvement in secular music from the start, Alexander was convinced that his backslidden state had caused his demise. When Memphis's WDIA planned a memorial broadcast of Ace's music following his death, Alexander called the station in vehement protest. The program was canceled.[16] Even those who lived hard and died young, however, got a glimpse of a material "Promised Land" that spelled the difference between poverty and privilege, between oppression and opportunity.

Until the 1950s, the perimeters of success for African Americans in any aspect of life were largely fixed by segregation. Marketing practices reflected the segregation of the larger society, as black music was aimed primarily, although not exclusively, at the black consumer. Even popular songs by white artists were routinely *covered* by black artists before they were issued in the then "Negro" market. In the 1940s, Dinah Washington was such a cover artist for Mercury Records, recording her own versions of preexisting pop tunes for distribution to black consumers. Few blacks owned record players in their homes during the 1940s, and any recording classified as a "hit" would most likely have been heard in black clubs where a jukebox was available. Even as late as 1954, a Columbia Records survey showed that only 50 percent of American families owned a phonograph. Through the early 1950s, most white pop deejays refused to play rhythm and blues, as the music still had a distinctively black sound. Artists like Dinah Washington were thus limited, to a large degree, by the glass ceiling of racial segregation.[17]

As segregation began to dissolve, blacks entertained hopes of fuller participation in all aspects of American life. Lured by the promise of a new social and economic order, greater numbers of church-trained black artists defected to the world of secular music in search of the American dream. For them, the dream was usually two-tiered. Their first goal was to successfully cross over from sacred music to rhythm and blues, a genre which, in the 1940s and early 1950s, was still primarily the domain of the black consumer. From there, an even greater accomplishment was to cross over from rhythm and blues to mainstream pop.[18]

While the defection of gospel artists from the church to the secular arena was pronounced in the 1950s, the seeds of this trend were actually planted decades earlier as societal changes induced a gradual weakening of church consciousness. The overall process of black America's "secularization," as Brian Ward calls it, extends back to the years of the early twentieth-century migration. During the 1920s and 1930s, the northern, black intelligentsia wrote about Race progress specifically in terms of detachment from a painful past of oppression and ignorance. These northern blacks were particularly critical of the folkways of their southern cousins who were arriving in droves to northern cities beginning in the late 1910s and 1920s. Their mannerisms, dialect, and religious customs were far too reminiscent of slavery, and in an effort to quickly induct the southern natives into a black, middle-class consciousness, the champions of Race pride called for a cultural amnesia, a purging of African-America's "primitive" memory. An editorial written in the February 1917 issue of the *Chicago Defender,* for example, urged black organizations to instruct the migrants in "proper" northern behavior. Michael Harris states: "Any migrant with the slightest disposition toward adopting new, northern ways was almost under a barrage of encouragement to do so."[19]

Drawings and editorials printed in the *Chicago Defender* made clear the desire of progressive blacks to move away from what they considered one of the most powerful reminders of the slave past: traditional folk religion. In 1921, the *Defender* included in its weekly segment titled "People We Can Get Along Without" a depiction of a jackleg preacher. In 1927, a letter to the editor captioned "Too Much Religion" stated that many blacks were victims of "a hypertheism superinduced by an inherent tendency to believe in the supernatural." Another letter published in the *Defender* in 1932 complained that "the Negro leans credulously toward 'conjure' men and 'spiritualists' . . . and is a chump for quackery." In the same year, another writer to the *Defender* commented that "the Negro Spiritual is overdone . . . we must remember that the observation of slaves in that period was limited, and because of extreme, oppressive servility, ignorance was rampant. . . ."[20]

As progressive blacks struggled to remove the stigma of religious extremism from their image, the larger society continued to portray blacks as woefully ignorant, yet, fanatically devout. A stereotypical portrayal of blacks and religion came with the opening of *The Green Pastures* in 1930. Written by white playwright Marc Connelly, the play features a black cast using slave dialect to deliver an ultra-ethnic, highly caricatured version of Biblical theology. The New York run of the play lasted from 1930 to 1931; it toured nationally from 1931 to 1932, was revived on stage in 1951, and made into a film in the 1950s. Progressive blacks deplored the damaging portrayal of African-American religion in *The Green Pastures,* and many, including elite members of the clergy, spoke out against its message which conveyed that religious blacks were inherently ignorant. Reverend W.H. Jernagin, president of the Fraternal Council of Negro Churches, stated that "the primitive religious concepts as portrayed in *The Green Pastures* which had its value in the past is no longer adequate for modern life. . . . Negroes demand more of their religion now," in particular, churches which address "common everyday problems and urgent needs."[21]

The years surrounding WWII brought another wave of southern-born blacks to the North and West. During this period, blacks continued in their efforts to present themselves as "New Negroes" evolved beyond their traditional dependence upon religion. In particular, the projects connected with the federal government's Intergroup Strategy underscore the intersection between race, religion, media, and image. In 1938 and 1939, the U.S. Office of Education presented a twenty-six week radio series entitled *Americans All, Immigrants All* as part of its Intergroup Strategy. In the wake of both the World War and ethnic tensions within its own populous, U.S. officials presented this program in an effort to promote an image of American national harmony and cohesiveness. Episodes in the series were devoted to the Italian, Irish, Mexican, and Asian immigrant groups, each of which were praised for their contributions to the highly idealized American utopia. Although the series was criticized for glossing over the cruel realities of immigrant life in America, it succeeded in awakening an awareness of cultural diversity in Americans whose lives were often segregated into homogenous, self-contained communities.

In particular, black leaders viewed *Americans All, Immigrants All* as a golden opportunity to erect before the nation an image of the Negro whose dignity would effectively counter the barrage of negative stereotypes force-fed to the American public since the early days of minstrelsy. For the episode of *Americans All* titled "The Negro," consultants Alain Locke and W.E.B. DuBois took great pains to scrutinize the script and extract all hints of stereotypical portrayal. It was much to their chagrin, therefore, that singer Jules Bledsoe had been recruited at the last minute to sing nine minutes' worth of a song entitled "Black Boy." Locke called the song an unforeseen "mammy interpolation," and the offensive line, "trust in the Lord and don't worry like the bees," conjured up the negative image of primitive blacks and their hyper-religiosity. In a stern letter of protest, Locke wrote that "the sentiment of the song was misrepresentative of contemporary Negro feeling and attitude."[22]

An example of the type of religious image that progressive blacks enthusiastically embraced is seen in the 1944 film *The Negro Soldier.* This film was produced by the War Department in an effort to ease race relations and to reassure black soldiers of their importance to the war effort. Carlton Moss, a young black writer, developed the script for the film, which was set in a black church. Black actors who auditioned for the role of the preacher were rejected because Moss felt that they were "too wedded to traditional depictions of African Americans." Eager to move as far as possible from the negative portrayal of *The Green Pastures,* Moss himself ultimately played the graceful, articulate preacher who narrates throughout the film.[23]

In *The Negro Soldier,* black religion is portrayed as stoic, intellectual, and humanistic. The preacher delivers not a soul-stirring sermon about the supernatural, the Bible, or the afterlife, but a thought-provoking lecture on the evils of communism. The parishioners are motionless, silent, and attentive. There is no singing, clapping, or shouting to ruffle the neatly coiffed hair, or the heavily starched, impeccable clothing. Although the film was out of sync with many realities of the black church at midcentury, it was widely accepted and praised because it portrayed religious blacks with intelligence, discipline, and dignity.

Before the black masses mobilized for civil rights in the 1950s, blacks believed that they could earn the respect and acceptance of the larger society by adapting an image compatible with white values. This belief is seen in the ideology of the Harlem Renaissance, during which composers like William Grant Still and Florence Price sought to "elevate" the race by casting ethnic musical materials in European forms, like the symphony and the sonata. African Americans were highly sensitive about the way whites perceived them, and their desire to be assessed favorably was the motivation for the hair straighteners and skin lighteners that pointed to the Negro standard of beauty in the 1930s and 1940s. An oft-printed ad in *Ebony* magazine during the 1940s even reads, "Your life would be brighter if your skin were lighter."

Blacks were not only self-conscious about their religious image, but they were also concerned about their dialect; their emulation of a "white" vocal quality was rather deliberate. A perfect example of this effort to earn respect and dignity through the use of "proper" dialect is the Negro segment of *Americans All, Immigrants All.* Barbara Dianne Savage writes:

> when one listens to the recorded versions of the script, the
> most obvious characteristic is the virtual absence of the use
> of dialect as a signifyer of black people, even in depictions
> of slaves. . . . Portrayals of Douglass and more contempo-
> rary figures were presented by black voices that were
> erudite and confident. The matter of the use of dialect had
> received careful attention . . . for example, in a section of
> the script on the Fisk Jubilee Singers, the stage direction
> specifically warned that "the following is spoken by
> Negroes with good education[;] approximate southern
> accent but not 'Stage Negro' type." . . . Ultimately, these
> directions about dialect represented broader decisions
> about what kind and what class of black people should be
> presented on the show, and to that extent . . . the show was
> an exemplary divergence from the usual radio depictions of
> black people.[24]

From the 1920s to the 1950s, the process of secularization oc- curred as blacks fought stereotypes of religious fanaticism, demanded more social and political responsiveness from their churches, and located for themselves opportunities afforded by the booming post-war economy. Hoping for mainstream acceptance, they worked to iron the ethnicity out of their voices and the stereotype of ignorance out of their religion. In particular, blacks were self-conscious about the more idiosyncratic features of African-American religion—spirit possession, the shout, emotional spontaneity—and they sought to put forth, instead, an image of black religion that the larger society would perceive as dignified, intelligent, and controlled. They moved further and further away from supernatural interpretations of life and adopted a more humanistic approach to questions of social, political, and economic destiny. The humanistic mind-set of the 1950s contrasts significantly with that of earlier generations of black Americans and helps to explain why blacks left the church for the secular stage during this period.

In the 1950s, optimistic blacks watched vestiges of segregation begin to crumble before their very eyes. One such stronghold was *Billboard*'s pop music chart, dedicated to the tracking of music in the white consumer market. When the Chords' "Sh-boom" traversed that racial barrier to become number one on the pop charts in 1954, many black artists read the event as a signal beckoning them to similar possibilities. Musically, "Sh-boom" contained virtually no hint of the black church aesthetic. There was no call-and-response, no hand-clapping, no flatted thirds or sevenths, no tambourines, no improvisation whatsoever. The familiar I–vi–ii–V "doo-wop" progression was the harmonic basis of this song, whose straightforward quadruple meter swings ever so subtly, drawing no particular attention to the offbeats. Not only was their music racially neutral, but the lyrics to "Sh-boom" were lighthearted, fun-loving, somewhat nonsensical, daydreamy, and smack-dab "middle-of-the-road." There was certainly no "black" dialect in "Sh-boom," and no reference to God or to the Devil. The closest that "Sh-boom" came to citing religion is a fleeting reference to "paradise up above," a common and timeless metaphor for romantic love. By perfecting a sound attuned to the mainstream aesthetic, the Chords had successfully crossed over into the dreamworld of white consumption. Conscious of white audiences, white tastes, and the rewards of crossing over, some of the most popular black artists in the mid to late 1950s and early 1960s embraced a musical style that downplayed or erased ethnic markers, thus becoming palatable to the mainstream. Songs like the Platters' "Only You," LaVern Baker's "Humpty Dumpty Heart," and Sam Cooke's "You Send Me" typify this vocal ideal.

Because the black church and its music had been so fundamental to the development of black secular artists of the 1950s, the conspicuous absence of church flavor or religious signifiers from so many black hits during this period is the very issue that demands commentary. The deliberate avoidance of church sound (i.e., emotional intensity, improvisatory flavor, call-and-response, syncopated rhythms, rhetorical exclamations like "Yes Lord!" etc.) suggests a deliberate avoidance of the stigma and stereotypes associated with black religion. In order to convey an image of sophistication and conformity to mainstream norms, these artists avoided or diluted the vocal and textual nuances that might conjure up the image of spirit possession in a Holiness revival meeting. This does not necessarily suggest that the Platters, Baker, Cooke, and others were ashamed of their religious heritages; instead, it suggests that they were highly conscious and cautious of the way these ethno-religious markers would be interpreted by the mainstream. There was a feeling among some blacks during this period that church music was the private cultural property of black people, a communal expression whose idiosyncratic meaning was best appreciated within the confines of the African-American community. Therefore, as they ascended the ladder of pop music success, they embraced the standard dialect, jargon, and musical aesthetic that whites understood. They used *correct* English, minimized their improvisation, ironed out their syncopation, choreographed their stage delivery, and sang songs of All-American, daydreamy optimism. Meanwhile, their ethno-religious identities were stored away in a completely separate compartment.

This assimilationist approach to black popular music in the 1950s and early 1960s, however, does not tell the entire story of artists who first sang in the church and later had secular careers. The 1950s was a highly volatile period, not only of social and political transition, but also of generational tension. While more conservative and middle-aged whites may have been more comfortable with the sanitized sounds of the Platters, white teenagers were receptive to the energy and ethnicity of black artists who retained their black gospel stylings

in their musical delivery. These young "rebels" recognized, appreciated, and even imitated unmistakably black sounds with huge doses
of charisma from the black church. Ray Charles, Little Richard, and
James Brown, for example, wedded church flavor to secular lyrics to
such an extent that regardless of a song's message, the gospel ethos
essentially remained intact. In fact, a substantial number of secular
tunes from the 1950s and 1960s were simply adaptations of preexisting gospel songs. Ben E. King's "Stand by Me" was adapted from
the gospel song, "Stand by Me, Father"; The Dominoes' "Have Mercy,
Baby" was adapted from "Have Mercy, Lord." Ray Charles made an
art form of the reappropriation. His "I Got a Woman," "Hallelujah, I
Love Her So," and "This Little Girl of Mine" were all adaptations of
gospel songs. Wilson Pickett's "Ninety-nine and a Half" borrowed
its lyrics from a gospel tune of the same name. And the lyrics to
Martha and the Vandellas' "Nowhere to Run" were also borrowed
from gospel.

As black artists and black music received unprecedented exposure and acceptance in the mainstream during the 1950s, some conservative blacks held fast to their traditional biases against the Devil's
music. A more significant indicator of the religious pulse of black
America during this period is the extent to which churchgoing blacks
actually supported and celebrated the gospel artists who were successful in the secular field. Sam Cooke's success, for example, depended to a large degree upon the continued loyalty of those who had
supported him in gospel. Even black clergymen, including the Reverend Charles Cooke, the Reverend C.L. Franklin, and the Reverend
John Alexander, father of Johnny Ace, supported and encouraged their
children's transition into secular music. Before the 1950s, the lines
between God and the Devil were so dogmatically (if not clearly)
drawn that religious consumers were never expected to patronize
secular music. By the 1950s, however, the tide had clearly changed,
a fact which suggests dramatically revised notions of good and evil
where black music was concerned.

The process of secularization begun decades earlier culminated
with urbanization and a change of the social focus of young blacks
from the church to recreational alternatives like radio, television,
records, dances, and concerts in the 1950s. Before the mass migra-

tion of blacks out of the South in the first half of the twentieth century, the church had a virtual monopoly on the social and moral structure of African-American life. When increasing numbers of blacks left southern country life for northern city life, the urban world offered secular alternatives for what had formerly been the function of the church. Brian Ward argues that for young black men, the street gang and its nonviolent counterpart, the street-corner vocal group, provided the sense of community and belonging that the church had once offered.[25] Black clergymen thus feared that these secular alternatives, including the music and the Saturday night excesses induced by it, would interfere with the teenagers' attendance at services on Sunday morning. A residual effect was the shrinking of audiences who provided a living for church-spawned gospel artists. One such artist, Brother Joe May, spoke out vehemently against rhythm and blues, calling it a fad and "nothing more than an offshoot of good gospel song."[26]

Just as urban culture competed with the centrality of the church in black life, the emerging Civil Rights Movement redefined its traditional function. In the 1950s, the black church became a meeting place for social awakening, and the faithful gathered there to organize a tangible salvation. In that setting, the Promised Land was not in the afterlife, but it was possible in the present life, complete with equal opportunity in housing, employment, and education. Whereas the black church of prior generations had focused on the segregation of saints from sinners and conversion of the latter, the church of the 1950s spawned a whole generation of preacher-activists who focused on integrating blacks into American society. Given its agenda of integration and activism for African Americans, the spiritual leadership of the black church softened its edict against secular music once the music came to symbolize social and economic opportunity for blacks. Even Martin Luther King stopped short of denouncing the music when he stated simply that "the profound sacred and spiritual meaning of the great music of the church must never be mixed with the transitory quality of rock and roll music."[27]

It is both ironic and highly symbolic of the times that Sam Cooke, a neophyte secular crooner, would record "That's Heaven to Me" in 1957 with the Soul Stirrers. In this recording, Cooke straddles more than one fence. He records this gospelesque piece with the Soul Stirrers during the same year that he achieves phenomenal pop success with "You Send Me." The lyrics of "That's Heaven to Me" teeter on the threshold between traditional black Christian theology and the social awareness that characterizes the progressive black church of the 1950s.

Cooke's definition of paradise in "That's Heaven to Me" resonates with the kind of paradise that activism was supposed to create: "The things that I see when I'm walking down the street / That's heaven to me. . . ." Cooke's secular sermonette promotes the image of a tangible, immediate heaven, and the song itself seems a defense of the route he chose for getting there.

In some respects, the socially conscious black church of the 1950s was the fulfillment of the fictional black church portrayed in *The Negro Soldier.* In both scenarios, social and political issues are at the foreground of the religious experience, while the supernatural dimension of black spirituality is less pronounced—even concealed.

Other factors notwithstanding, the most potent attraction to secular music in the 1950s was money. Gospel performers and sacred quartet singers in the 1940s and 1950s could expect a wide range of compensation for their services, depending upon their experience, professionalism, and popularity with their constituencies. In the early days of gospel and sacred quartet singing, performances were not commercial in nature. According to Ray Allen, author of *Singing in the Spirit,* "usually a free will offering would be taken and split fifty-fifty between the groups and the sponsoring church."[28] Allen quotes Charlie Storey, a quartet singer in New York in the 1940s, who states: "Back then, more groups sang for free. They'd come and help your church, and your church would come back and help their church. That's the way they did it. Nobody said nothing about money in those days. When you spoke about some money, about getting paid, that was like a bad word—a curse word. They might take us up an offering, but whatever they raised, you didn't say nothing."[29]

At the same time that literally thousands of amateur artists and groups continued to subsist on freewill offerings during the heyday of gospel music, many others rode the tidal wave of financial opportunity by becoming semiprofessional or full-time professional sa-

cred artists. Allen states: "After the second World War, gospel music
. . . rose to new commercial heights. Its popularity was fueled by an
expanding radio and recording industry, a well established touring
circuit, and a growing black urban population that could afford to
support professional singers."[30] Kip Lornell describes the financial
interests and operations of gospel quartets and groups during the 1940s
and 1950s:

> Finances became an even greater factor as the business end
> of quartet singing grew more lucrative and stakes in-
> creased. Programs headlined by major groups usually
> included three or four other local or regionally recognized
> acts and brought in thousands of dollars in a single night.
> Multistar events, sometimes known as caravans, included
> as many as three or four big names. . . . These big-money
> programs took place in major venues of big cities like New
> York City's Apollo Theater or Birmingham's Civic Cen-
> ter. . . . During the program itself they also encouraged fans
> to buy some of the merchandise, usually records and
> autographed photographs, of the each of the groups [sic].
> No doubt about it, this was a lucrative enough business that
> each member of the quartet carefully scrutinized all of the
> financial transactions.[31]

The lucrative potential of gospel music during this period is further underscored by the first million-selling recordings in the genre:
Mahalia Jackson's rendition of "Move on Up a Little Higher," recorded in 1947; and Clara Ward's "Surely, God Is Able," recorded in
1949.

By 1955, gospel quartets had reached the peak of their commercial success. The major quartets amassed substantial earnings through
touring and personal appearances, and other gospel singers, including Brother Joe May, the Clara Ward singers, and Roberta Martin,
had financial security sufficient to enable them to spend their lives
advancing the cause of gospel music through performance, promotion, and composition. Lornell states that "A spirit of commercialism and showmanship pervaded all of black American gospel music

as everyone tried to catch their share of the money and the glory generated by this intense, widespread interest."[32]

While black sacred artists in the 1940s and 1950s were far from poor, their earnings paled in comparison to those of their secular counterparts. By 1950, the signals were quite clear: A successful gospel artist could live well, but a successful secular artist could live far better. Daniel Wolff notes that the Soul Stirrers grossed $78,000 in 1953. Wolff observes, however, that "On Christmas weekend, 1954, [Alan] Freed's show at the Academy Theater grossed $125,000—more in one weekend than the Stirrers had earned the entire previous year!" An even greater disparity could be cited between gospel celebrities and black artists in the popular mainstream, like Nat King Cole, who, by 1956, was earning $83,000 a week.[33]

Professional gospel artists stood to earn considerably more money by becoming professional secular artists. For the amateur gospel singer with no stage experience beyond the pulpit of his own church, the financial possibilities were no less attractive. The 1950 census showed the median income of blacks in Memphis, Atlanta, Birmingham, and New Orleans to be around $980 annually. By 1953, twenty-four-year-old Johnny Ace was earning an estimated $600 per night as a secular singer. For average black Americans, this earning potential was unprecedented and encouraged a wholesale rethinking of the traditional association of the Devil and secular music.[34]

Another factor influencing gospel artists to cross over to secular music was the emergence of a new breed of white entrepreneurs seeking to capitalize on black talent. Whites have always played an integral role in the popularization of black music. At a time when segregation and institutionalized racism excluded blacks from economic opportunities, whites provided access to the capital and the contacts needed for the recording, marketing, and distribution of black music. Although black artists were certainly exploited in this process, the music's dissemination and availability for widespread consumption was fostered to a large degree by white entrepreneurial prowess and white financial resources. In many respects, "entrepreneurial prowess" could be read as "racial exploitation," as the inequities of covering and other unethical practices bear out. But not all whites were racist opportunists out to make a fast buck. Some, like

John Hammond, appear to have been genuinely philanthropic. Hammond was born into wealth, his mother having been an heiress to the Vanderbilt fortune and his father a mercantile tycoon. Hammond's decision to associate with blacks earned him persecution from both his family and from the larger society, and his professional interest in jazz went totally opposite the grain of acceptable vocations in his family. Disillusioned by the social order of his upbringing and incensed by the treatment of blacks, Hammond claims to have chosen to champion the music of blacks as an "effective and constructive form of social protest." Hammond said, "The times themselves imposed insurmountable odds, particularly for Negroes, against achieving any sort of recognition without help. The opportunities for me were clear."[35]

Both black and white record executives persuaded many gospel performers to cross over to secular music. According to Sam Cooke, Bumps Blackwell constantly prodded him to go pop. Blackwell even admitted that he and Cooke, who initially feared losing his religious audience, argued over the matter. Tulsan J.W. Alexander scouted gospel groups for Art Rupe's Specialty label to record, but was ever on the lookout for crossover talent that might interest Bumps Blackwell. When Blackwell left Specialty for Keen records, Keen sought to capitalize on Blackwell's ties to black gospel artists. Fred Smith, an employee of Keen, notes that during that time, "the gospel field was beginning to be recognized as a major source for r&b singers."[36] Art Rupe gave his record company the name Specialty because he wanted to specialize in "citified Negro music" with a big-band sound "expressed in a churchy way. . . ."[37] In fact, the roster of former church-singers-turned-celebrity who were connected to Rupe or Blackwell is impressive: In addition to Cooke, Jesse Belvin, Lou Rawls, and Little Richard all had connections to these producers. Not only did Bumps Blackwell try to persuade Cooke to go pop, but so did Bob Schiffman, owner of the Apollo Theater.

While white record executives appreciated the church flavor that many black artists brought to the secular arena, fundamental cultural differences between blacks and whites often prevented the latter from a genuine understanding of the spiritual motivation behind gospel performance, however secularized the music may have become by the 1950s. Randy Wood, the white president of Vee Jay Record Company beginning in 1962, stated rather bluntly: "I can handle gospel, not intellectually, but musically. Intellectually, it's a bunch of bullshit, as far as I am concerned. But the nuances and the approach to music of The Staple Singers is fantastic. They have managed to bridge the gap. They have taken what is fundamentally a gospel sound and given it pop appeal—those rhythm patterns, the reading of the lyrics (grassroots mentality) when it comes out of your speaker, it's something that doesn't identify itself as to color; it bridges all the gaps."[38] At least a few African Americans viewed the charismatic gospel experience with a similar mixture of mockery, fascination, and disdain. Bumps Blackwell, who ultimately succeeded in persuading Sam Cooke to pursue pop success, describes what he observed in one of Cooke's pre-pop gospel performances: "People were screaming, throwing purses, and umbrellas and stick-pins. You were liable to get yourself killed! It was awesome, phenomenal: He was like a black Billy Graham. Shit, the girls were following him around like the pied piper. Girls and young guys, musicians, but the chicks would just be completely gone."[39]

The typical, cultural response of blacks to gospel music is conditioned by and deeply rooted in the African-born tradition of spirit possession. Black worshippers commonly allow sacred music to fill them with such inspiration that physical expression becomes a natural response. Dancing, screaming, and fainting are not at all unusual in these settings. Thoroughly rooted in the folk-religious traditions of the black experience, gospel music had little in common with the liturgical background of the average Anglo-American. To a white onlooker in the 1950s, therefore, such responses might have seemed both foreign and chaotic. And given Sam Cooke's physical attractiveness, it might have been natural for those with a more formal religious background to misinterpret such responses to Cooke as sexually motivated theatrics. Although the spiritual basis of black gospel performance may have been widely misunderstood, the lucrative potential in this kind of audience reaction was clear, and recording industry stakeholders sought to exploit it. As church-trained artists embarked upon secular careers, they, too, were in deliberate pursuit of progress and prosperity.

In the 1950s, crossing over from gospel to secular music symbolized the traversal of several boundaries. It was a passage from the segregated past into an integrated future, the passage from a religious life focus to a humanistic mindset, and the passage from economic limitations to seemingly infinite economic possibilities. Crossing over from gospel to secular music was the official, ceremonial rejection of the belief that rhythm and blues and pop were the Devil's domain. It was an assertive departure from the religious assumptions and constraints of earlier generations.

While the de-churchified sounds of black pop artists typified the late 1950s and early 1960s, by the mid-1960s black consumers were signaling that a change in musical preference was on the horizon. The desire among blacks for integration and full participation in American society was beginning to crumble beneath the weight of harsh realities. By around 1963, violence, instability, and political and economic disappointments forced many blacks to rethink the plausibility of integration.

For the Platters, this reality check came on August 10, 1959, when the group's four male members were arrested at a hotel in Cincinnati for allegedly consorting with prostitutes, who happened to be white. The incident resulted in an immediate loss of concert bookings and radio support. While the case was eventually dismissed, many believed that the Platters had been the targets of racism.

Throughout the late 1950s and early 1960s, the boundaries between "white" sounds and "black" sounds had become so muddled that in November 1963 *Billboard* published what it believed would be its last rhythm-and-blues chart. By January 1965, however, *Billboard* responded to the signals of black consumers by resurrecting, once again, a chart to track music that, unlike the crossover sounds of the late 1950s, was distinctively black. This music was the expression of an emerging sentiment of disillusionment among young African Americans, and they underscored black identity in the music by reincorporating the sounds and signifiers of the black church into secular material—the same elements that had been extracted just a few years prior in an effort to assimilate into the mainstream.

The ascendancy of Curtis Mayfield was perhaps the most potent example of this re-churchification of black secular sound. Mayfield had inherited potent church training from his preacher-grandmother, who was pastor of the Traveling Soul Spiritualist Church in Chicago. His music made no apologies for its heavy doses of traditional black spirituality. His "People Get Ready" of 1964, for example, borrows heavily from the characteristic themes and metaphors of the Negro spiritual: "People get ready, there's a train a comin'." . . ." Metaphors of traveling and of water occur repeatedly in Negro spirituals, and they symbolize motion from the present life to a better life. In "People Get Ready," Mayfield taps into the spiritual memory of black America and resurrects a poetic device so deeply grounded in the sacred music tradition of black America that its implications are hard to miss. For anyone unsure that this is church music, Mayfield's lyrics cite the Lord directly.

When blacks favored integration, they extracted religious signifiers from their popular music in an effort to *fit in* with the rest of America. As blacks abandoned the ideal of integration, they reincorporated church elements into their music as a way to embrace, distinguish, and celebrate their cultural, racial, and ethnic identity. Even Motown, black music's icon of crossover and assimilation, used church flavor as a prominent feature of its music in the mid-1960s. Jon Fitzgerald's analysis of over sixty Motown hits between 1963 and 1966 shows that such gospel features as the verse/chorus format, short repeated refrains, blues and pentatonic scales, and syncopated chord changes are prominent and recurring features.[40] Sam Cooke also reclaimed gospel flavoring in "A Change Is Gonna Come." Recorded in 1964, the song bears a resemblance to "Pilgrim of Sorrow."[41] In the late 1960s and early 1970s, the flavor of the black church returns full force in the music of Solomon Burke, the Staple Singers, Aretha Franklin, and others. This thorough re-churchification of black secular music not only signals the social and political sentiments of blacks during that time, but also shows a new willingness on the part of blacks to display the fusion of their sacred and secular identities without apology or compromise. More important, perhaps, it shows that traditional concepts of good and evil, of sanctity and sin, and God and the Devil had been irrevocably altered.

5

EVOLUTION OF THE BLUES PREACHER

Sermonizing Modes in Black Secular Music

In African-American culture, it is common for vocal artists to divide their professional lives between the pulpit and secular performance. Many blues singers, for example, were also men and women of the cloth—reverends, ministers, and evangelists representing a variety of persuasions. Blues artist Johnny Watson (1867–1963) toured with minstrel troupes, medicine shows, and Zydeco bands and recorded on several labels. At the same time, he worked under the pseudonym "Reverend Alfred Pitts," when performing gospel music. The Reverend Blind Gary Davis (1896–1972) sang and preached the gospel on the streets, in churches, and on the "chittlin' circuit." He not only evangelized, but recorded prolifically, and his output includes "Baby Let Me Lay It on You," "Cocaine Blues," and "Sally, Where'd You Get the Liquor From?" Tim Wilkins, a.k.a., Reverend Robert Wilkins (b. 1896–1987), played with jugbands and at juke joints, performing with the likes of Gus Cannon, Furry Lewis, and others. In 1950 he became an ordained minister in the Church of God in Christ, after which he recorded religious material but also toured extensively with blues and folk festivals throughout the United States. Blind Lemon Jefferson (1897–1929) was an itinerant singer and guitarist performing the blues at brothels, saloons, and barrel houses in the South and Midwest. Using at times the pseudonym "Deacon L.J. Bates," and, at other times, the pseudonym "Elder J.C. Brown," Blind Lemon performed and recorded religious material. Josephine Miles (c. 1900–c. 1953–1965) performed with the company of *Shuffle Along* in the 1920s and recorded on nearly a half dozen labels while in New York City. She was also Evangelist Mary Flowers and was reportedly involved in church work from some time in the 1930s until her death. The Reverend Rubin Lacy (1902–c. 1972) performed the blues throughout Mississippi and the Midwest and accompanied many blues artists on a variety of labels, including Columbia and Paramount. His output also includes the sacred material he recorded after becoming an ordained minister in the Baptist church. Other blues artists who worked in the ministry include Joe McCoy (1905–1950), a.k.a., "Hallelujah Joe," Johnny Williams (b. 1906), a.k.a., "Reverend Johnny Williams," Arnold "Gatemouth" Moore (b. 1913), and Pinewood Tom (1915–1969) a.k.a., Joshua White, "The Singing Christian." For many of these artists, work in the ministry was retribution for a life spent singing "the Devil's music." For others, however, the ministry and the blues hailed from a common inspiration.[1]

This simultaneous call to preaching the gospel and singing the blues underscores a uniquely African-American approach to the sacred/secular dichotomy. In this approach, the sacred and the secular, while separate in theory, are frequently combined in practice. Where strict separation between sacred and secular is valued, the preacher who both proclaims the gospel and sings the blues is a troublesome anomaly. The apparent contradiction in this dual identity may not be a contradiction at all but rather two different facets of a single cultural function, perhaps traceable to the *griot* of West Africa.

In African societies, the griot is a specialist in the spoken word. He functions as storyteller, genealogist, reporter, advisor, herald, social commentator, and professional flatterer or insulter. Griots are also master singers and musicians who typically play instruments (most commonly, a lute-like instrument called the *kora*) in accompaniment to their discourse. A professional caste, griots occupy a position separate and distinct from the rest of society. As the guardians of genealogy, griots enjoy access to influential political positions, serving as advisers to heads of state. Their social status can be ambiguous in that they are simultaneously considered both leaders and servants. Their leadership capacity results from their special clearance to wield influence, while the servanthood is carried out in the communicative responsibilities and tasks they perform for the community. Because of their unique function, griots "enjoy almost complete freedom of expression, behavior, and movement. They are bound neither by etiquette, nor by the community's rules of common law, nor by most religious taboos."[2]

While Western culture has no direct equivalent of the African griot, certain parallels between the griot and the black-American preacher are clear. During the antebellum era, the black preacher emerged as a leadership figure who, like the griot, was considered both an elder of and a servant to the slave community. Whether male or female, the slave preacher occupied a position of respect and authority, and blacks and whites alike recognized the preacher as the primary mouthpiece of his fellow bondsmen. As did the griot, the antebellum slave preacher relied upon oral tradition to transmit information through story, sermon, and song. Speaking of slave religious leaders, Stacey Close writes that "Much of what the leaders learned had to be memorized over the years." Describing a slave preacher named Old Uncle Jack, Close notes that "Jack could not read or write; yet his knowledge of religious matters resulted from his conversing and sharing his views with other knowledgeable persons."[3]

Black religious leadership on the plantation went beyond the sermonizing skill of the slave preacher. The religious leader was also expected to mobilize his followers toward spirit possession, since this type of ecstasy provided much needed catharsis and temporary escape from a harsh reality. The religious leadership in the slave community also used his voice for social commentary, frequently to his own detriment. Close writes: "The slave preacher . . . had to be sure not to preach a gospel of freedom that whites might overhear. Sarah Ford (ex-slave) reported that Uncle Lew spoke to an audience about unity and equality of whites and blacks. The owner moved Uncle Lew into the fields because of his statements. An old preacher, Uncle Tom Ewing, once spoke the words 'freed indeed, free from work, free from the white folks, free from everything' in the presence of his owner and found himself threatened with not being allowed to preach."[4]

The slave preacher was often recognized for his ability to sing, and congregants depended on his musical leadership during worship. In 1937, a former slave recounted her baptismal experience to an interviewer with the Federal Writer's Project, and in so doing she made reference to the slave preacher's musical role. She recalled that "the banks of Austin's pond was lined with Negroes shouting and singing glory and praises. They sang all the songs they could think of, and the preacher lined out songs to them."[5] Another former slave stated: "We was always compelled to go to church. Boss like for de slaves to sing while workin'. We had a jack-leg slave preacher who'd hist de tunes."[6] During camp meetings and revivals, slave preachers were inspired to compose songs extemporaneously, which were then repeated and embellished by the congregation.

In congregations of free blacks, the religious leadership took responsibility for the musical life of the church. Richard Allen, founder of the African Methodist Episcopal Church, compiled a hymnal for his congregation, which included some of his own compositions.[7] It is likely that Allen taught these hymns to his church members.

The ability to inform, to exhort, to influence, and to sing are qualities that the black preacher of antebellum times shared with the griot of West Africa. And although the black preacher evolved within Western society and was shaped, to a significant degree, by the West's tendency to polarize the sacred and the secular, he continued—in practice if not in conviction—to function in both realms.

While volumes have been produced on the black preacher in the church, little has been written on the black preacher in secular music. As do those who function exclusively within the church, the black preachers resident in secular music inform, exhort, and influence their faithful, proselytizing for their belief systems and at times invoking the supernatural for a desired effect.

A single definition of the black preacher is difficult to come by, for as Charles Hamilton asserts, they "cover the spectrum, from pimps to paragons, riches to rags, radicals to reactionaries, scholars to charlatans."[8] In media, in literature, in theater, and in music, images of the black preacher range from the ignorant, jackleg profiteer to the educated activist/martyr. The preacher is the first and oldest leadership role in black-American culture, and the vast majority of African

An African-American preacher exhorts his congregation. (Photo courtesy of the Curtis Humphrey Photograph Collection, Texas African American Photography Archive, Documentary Arts, Inc., Dallas, Texas)

Americans consider his responsibilities to be both spiritual and social in nature. This fact is confirmed in a 1987 study by James H. Harris which shows black America's three primary expectations of the black preacher. Of the 338 respondents polled, 78 percent indicated that they expected for the black preacher to demonstrate active concern for the oppressed; 68.5 percent indicated that they expected the black preacher to demonstrate aggressive political leadership; and 60.25 percent indicated that they expected the black preacher to evangelize through proclamation of the Gospel.[9] These findings are significant because they suggest that, at least by the 1980s, most African Americans expected for the preacher's work to be carried out in places other than from behind the pulpit.

Although most African Americans hail from Christian backgrounds, these statistics also indicate that blacks consider proclamation of the Gospel to be the least important of the black preacher's primary functions. But that is not to say that blacks consider this an insignificant function. Harris's study simply indicates that it is not as important to blacks as the other two responsibilities. Blacks are far less concerned with the preacher's grasp of the doctrinal tenets of Christianity than they are with his ability to mobilize the community toward positive change. For the purpose of this discussion, therefore, I consider black preachers to include those who champion other "gospels," including Islam and Egyptology. It's important to consider non-Christian perspectives in this discussion because of the change in black religious consciousness that came about after the Civil Rights Movement. In their search for Afrocentricity, many blacks abandoned the faith of their upbringings and explored religious alternatives to Christianity, alternatives which they felt bore a more salient connection to their ethnicity. Religious themes in the black secular music of the 1970s reference these spiritual alternatives to a degree never seen before. Statistics from a study published in 1977 by H. Beecher Hicks Jr. point to a decline in the Christian indoctrination of black Americans. Of the 212 respondents who answered a question about church attendance, 47 percent said that while they attended church frequently in childhood, they rarely attended as adults.[10]

The black preachers of secular music represent spiritual persuasions ranging from traditional Christianity to Egyptology. Some proselytize through their performances, and others maintain a distinction between their secular and spiritual roles, switching hats, as it were, whenever needed. Despite the many modes through which these preachers reconcile their spirituality with their music, they all claim a divine call to enlighten, educate, and inspire those who patronize them.

Black preachers have been active in secular music since the blues era. During this time, artists traversed the sacred/secular divide through the use of pseudonyms. The purpose of the pseudonym was not to conceal the identity of the artist, since the listening public would have known perfectly well that Blind Lemon Jefferson and Deacon L.J. Bates were the same person. Instead, because of the cultural strictures that forbade the deliberate mingling of the sacred with the secular, the artist used the pseudonym to indicate his or her allegiance—at least for the duration of the recording. When working for the Lord, the artist usually went by Reverend, Deacon, Elder, Evangelist, or Minister; when working for the Devil, as it were, the artist assumed a more commonplace identity, frequently a nickname designed to endear him to the average sinner.

Although many black artists in the early part of the twentieth century felt it necessary to use the pseudonyms when switching sides, in many cases, there was actually very little stylistic difference between early black sacred and secular recordings. Particularly in the 1920s, many black artists, whether singing sacred lyrics or secular ones, exhibit a generic folk style characterized by vernacular dialect and self-accompaniment on guitar or some other instrument. During the early 1900s, the guitar was still considered by many blacks to be the Devil's instrument, and perhaps for this reason even religious songs with such folk-guitar accompaniment are classified as blues, although the terms "holy blues" and "preaching blues" might reference those with sacred texts.

One preacher who sings his sermon in this generic, African-American folk style is Washington Phillips, and his "Denomination Blues," recorded in 1927, is rendered in two parts, both released during the same year. In the lyrics, Phillips bemoans the complexity of denominationalism and comments on the idiosyncrasies of the Baptists, the Methodists, the Presbyterians, and others. His discourse is punctuated with the refrain, "But you got to have Jesus, that's all." Little is known of Phillips's life, but, as was typical of those associated in any way with the blues, Phillips seems to have been somewhat detached from mainstream church life, as his diatribes against religious denominationalism suggest. At the same time, his refrain, "You've got to have Jesus," underscores his personal conviction and the potency of his own spirituality.

That Phillips uses a dolceola instead of a guitar to accompany himself on these recordings is interesting. The dolceola was a stringed instrument invented in the 1890s by an Ohio piano tuner named David Boyd. This portable instrument had a rather ethereal sound, and its timbre was part guitar, part mandolin. Documents suggest that less than a hundred were produced.[11] Although no one knows how Washington Phillips was able to obtain a dolceola (especially since the instrument was invented in Ohio and Phillips recorded "Denomination Blues" in Dallas, Texas), it is possible that he chose this instrument as an alternative to the guitar, which had strong secular associations. The dolceola may well have been Phillips's way to avoid accusations of "straddling the fence" between God and the Devil.

Religious assertions like those heard in "Denomination Blues" mellowed as blacks during the mid-century years became more inclined to keep their religion and their recreational music separate. This tendency may well have come with the change in black social life resulting from massive northward migration. As increasing numbers of blacks moved to the North and to the city, they encountered recreational alternatives that competed with the centrality of the church. In the 1930s, 1940s, and early 1950s, the religious themes that surfaced in black popular music were very likely to emerge in the context of humor, parody, or satire. During these years, Louis Jordan, the Dominoes, Little Esther Phillips, and others recorded a whole repertoire of humorous "deacon" tunes which highlighted the seedier facets of the black preacher's image. While religious themes gave humor to these secular songs, *serious* religious sentiment was considered inappropriate for entertainment. It is precisely for this reason that Rosetta Tharpe met with such hot criticism from blacks when she attempted to maintain a churchgoing identity in an entertainment venue. In the end, she, too, was perceived as humorous.

During the mid-1950s, when most blacks held fast to high hopes for integration and equality, religious declarations were virtually nonexistent in the black secular styles which aimed toward becoming mainstream. During the days of doo-wop and crossover, the preacher persona in secular music was submerged beneath the group identities of early rhythm and blues. Named for birds and cars, the young black artists of the doo-wop era traveled in packs, content to contribute their individual voices and talents to the artistic unit. Solo artists like Sam Cooke supplanted the preacher persona with mainstream, mellow crooning, lighthearted lyrics, and polished presentation. Where "crossing over" was key, religious zeal was unacceptable. Those who hoped to appeal to white audiences crossed over the divide separating not only the white aesthetic from the black aesthetic but also the strictly sacred from the strictly secular. Becoming mainstream meant either diluting the idiosyncrasies of black religion or leaving them in the church where they "belonged."

By the early 1960s, hopes for full-fledged integration were fad-ing, and once-idealistic blacks were becoming disillusioned in the wake of several specific events. In 1963 alone, Medgar Evers was assassinated, Birmingham's Sixteenth Street Baptist Church was bombed, killing four little black girls, and President Kennedy was killed while campaigning in Dallas. A full ten years after *Brown* v. *Board of Education,* the "deliberate speed" with which school desegregation was mandated had proven alarmingly slow. In 1964, only 2 percent of black children in the South were attending integrated schools.[12] In 1965, conflict between black citizens and white police officers in Los Angeles escalated into the Watts riot, the most devastating racial disturbance in U.S. history at that time. Disillusioned by what many considered a failed Civil Rights Movement and no longer aspiring toward mainstream acceptance, many blacks returned to their own cultural roots for validation.

In the 1960s, as the focus of young blacks switched from integration to revolution, religious themes resurfaced in black secular music with a vengeance. With artists like Curtis Mayfield, Aretha Franklin, and James Brown, there was an unabashed reclaiming of the gospel

Aretha Franklin
(Author's collection)

ethos, not just for its aesthetic appeal, but as a specific symbol of black identity. There was also a reclaiming and a celebration of the preacher persona, as black secular artists freely borrowed their lyrics, their vocal styles, and their physical gestures from the African-American pulpit.

In particular, Curtis Mayfield brought a religious revival to black popular music. Mayfield was born and raised in Chicago where his grandmother pastored the Traveling Soul Spiritualist Church. As a child, he sang with the Northern Jubilee Gospel Choir but was still a teenager when he formed his first rhythm-and-blues group, the Alphatones. A second group, the Roosters, went through several transitions and eventually evolved into the Impressions, the Soul group for which Mayfield served as lead singer, guitarist, and songwriter. The distinguishing feature of Mayfield's music was its delivery of political and inspirational messages adorned in the style, feeling, jargon, and gestures of the black church. As messenger, Mayfield's preaching heritage becomes evident. He states that "My heart and soul came from my early days in the church. My grandmother was a preacher and it was through her that many of my song ideas came about."[13] In this statement, Mayfield stops short of claiming to have received the call himself. Describing the agenda of his music, Mayfield states: "Our purpose is to educate as well as to entertain. Painless preaching is as good a term as any for what we do."[14] Songs like "People Get Ready," "Amen," "Keep on Pushing," and "We're a Winner" echo the spirited exhortation frequently associated with the black preacher.

In "People Get Ready," Mayfield invokes the type of imagery common to the Negro spiritual. In the spiritual, nineteenth-century blacks used metaphors of traveling to express the idea of passage from despair to hope in the afterlife. Because of the importance of the railroad in the nineteenth century, blacks during this period used the metaphor of a moving train in their songs to convey the sense of passage through life on the way to heaven. In addition, references to Biblical bodies of water in the Negro spiritual (the river Jordan, the Red Sea) usually symbolized important barriers or boundaries to be traversed. In Mayfield's 1965 hit, the lyrics "People get ready, there's a train a comin' / don't need no baggage, just get on board" conjure up a familiar, church-specific use of imagery that many blacks, particularly those from the Baptist and Pentecostal traditions, would have readily associated, not only with any number of sacred songs but also with the colorful and poetic sermonizing tradition of the black preacher. Dolan Hubbard writes that, historically, the task of the black preacher has been to "invite his spatially immobile community to join him in creating a new world by transcending the narrow confines of the one in which they were forced to live. . . . Through his magnificently wrought oral poetry, the unlettered and semiliterate black preacher, in . . . moving the people from *here* to *there*, moves the spirit of the people beyond the boundary of hierarchical social order to the creation of new forms of human consciousness."[15] This is *exactly* the role that Mayfield assumes when, from the technological pulpit, he tells his virtual congregation to prepare for the approaching metaphorical train, in essence, to anticipate motion from *here* to *there*. As we shall see, the black preachers of non-Christian gospels also perform this function as they use music to create places of consciousness that transcend the confines of here and now.

In addition to its use of this imagery, "People Get Ready" employs the call-and-response device so intrinsic to traditional black church life. While call-and-response is frequently associated with the hand-clapping, foot-stomping exuberance of folk worship (a fine example of which is the Impressions' "Amen"), its presence in "People Get Ready" is a tad more subtle. With a vocal style that might be described as plaintively beautiful, Mayfield begins a line ("People get ready . . .) which is then completed (". . . get on board") by his ensemble of backup singers. Neither his use of familiar imagery, nor his somewhat subdued use of call-and-response in "People Get Ready" would have been lost on blacks in 1965.

During that critical period, "People Get Ready" functioned in several important ways. With its use of elements specific to black religious culture, it was a coded call for solidarity, pointing blacks toward a spiritual ideal *despite* overwhelming social and political malaise. The song brought familiar elements of black religious tradition out of the closet, as it were, and thrust them into secular consciousness. Most important, perhaps, is the fact that "People Get Ready" represents the revival of the preaching tradition in black secular music that had been practically dormant since the days of the early twentieth-century blues preachers. Mayfield's message songs paved the way for others to infuse secular music with their own moral and inspirational exhortations. Because his music spoke so directly to the sentiment of those turbulent times, Mayfield effectively dissolved the barrier between the sacred and secular and brought a certain respectability to the practice of preaching from the entertainment pulpit.

Mayfield's clear political and inspirational agenda invites an interesting comparison to that of his contemporary, Solomon Burke. There is some uncertainty about the date of Burke's birth, which has been cited as 1935, 1936, or 1940.[16] According to Burke, the confusion about his birth year results from his appearance to his grandmother in a dream twelve years before his physical arrival. Convinced that Burke was destined for spiritual leadership, Burke's grandmother founded a church, The House of God for All People. While still a youngster, Burke assumed leadership of the church, also called "Solomon's Temple." He was seven years old when he delivered his first sermon, and by the ripe age of nine was evangelizing as the Wonder Boy Preacher. Before he was a teenager, he had a radio ministry and was leading weekend tent revivals in the southeastern states.[17]

It appears that from the very beginning, Burke was destined not just for the ministry but for the spotlight. His birth having been foretold and his arrival eagerly anticipated by his grandmother and his mother (also an ordained minister), Burke never knew a time when he was not the center of attention. If either 1935 or 1936 is taken to be the actual year of his birth, then Burke was not quite twenty years old when he started recording secular sides for the Apollo label in 1955. He was introduced to Apollo by a Philadelphia deejay who heard him sing during a gospel talent contest.

Early on, Burke felt the conflict between his attraction to secular music on the one hand and his allegiance to the church on the other. To say that he was "torn," however, would be something of an overstatement. Burke states: "I was always of the church, and once in grace, always in grace. . . . I don't smoke, I don't drink, and I believe very strongly in my religious beliefs, so I refused to be classified as a rhythm-and-blues singer. In those days, that was a stigma of profanity."[18] Classification notwithstanding, Burke *was* a rhythm-and-blues singer with a string of hits to prove it, including "Just Out of Reach," "Cry to Me," and "The Price." In the end, Burke decided that secular music was not the antithesis of the church but, rather, "a new avenue, a new dimension to spread the gospel."[19]

Whatever his views about God or about the social order, Burke's mode of sermonizing on his secular recordings is confined primarily to the aesthetic level. The lyrics to his most popular recordings are addressed to his romantic interests, not to any virtual congregation. "Just Out of Reach (Of My Two Open Arms)" was released on Atlantic in 1961 and sounds more like Elvis than like gut-wrenching Soul music, yet, it was number seven on the rhythm-and-blues charts and number twenty-four on the pop charts. This country-and-western ballad is highly symbolic of a period during which stakeholders in the music business were obsessed with crossing over. Burke successfully appealed to white consumers by using tidy tone quality, minimal improvisation, and standard, middle-American dialect. The song contains a spoken interlude which is rehearsed, measured, perhaps even borderline Shakespearean.[20]

By the time he released "Cry to Me" in 1962, Burke the preacher (both literally and figuratively) had loosened his collar, rolled up his sleeves, and let himself go. In Burke's most popular recordings from 1962 onward, elements of the African-American folk-preaching style are salient. One of the elements is the fusion of speech and song. Speech-song results when the preacher's spoken discourse takes on a melodic/rhythmic character that accentuates the phrase structure and the semantic contour of the homily. In a typical church setting, the preacher's speaking voice may evolve into the speech-song and intensify as he approaches the climax of his sermon. It is also typical for the speech-song to become part of a call-and-response exchange between preacher and congregation. The preacher delivers a phrase, to which the congregation responds with various expressions of praise, agreement, or approval ("Hallelujah!" "Yes Sir!" "Yes, Lord!"). This extemporaneous exchange between preacher and congregation continues until the devotional ends of the church service are satisfied.

Another element in the oratorical style of the black folk preacher is the use of repetition or elongation for emphasis. The preacher may elongate or repeat a particular phrase, word, syllable, consonant, or vowel. These devices are used to emphasize particular points or ideas, and they force the congregation to consider and reconsider both the sound and the sense of what is said and thus to absorb the full meaning and impact of the utterance. Finally, the folk preacher improvises hollers and vocal melismas, both in dialogue with the congregation and in response to spiritual ecstasy.

In contrast to the restraint of "Just out of Reach," Burke's later recordings, including "Down in the Valley" (1962), "I'm Hanging up My Heart for You" (1962), "If You Need Me" (1963), and "You're Good for Me" (1963), exhibit these folk-preaching characteristics. Near the end of "Cry to Me," for example, Burke isolates and repeats the word *cry* in such a way that it takes on a percussive quality. "I'm Hanging up My Heart for You," which includes an organ in its instrumentation, sounds churchy enough for any Sunday morning service. In particular, when Burke sings, "I wanna thank you—yes, I wanna thank you for making me see the light," it is not altogether clear whether Burke is thanking the Lord or the hypothetical woman to whom he is singing. "You're Good for Me" ends with a monologue containing Burke's masterful use of the speech-song technique. Don Covay, a songwriter and close associate of Burke's, states that "Solomon wouldn't record without his pulpit in the studio."[21] Burke himself claimed that during a concert in England, his show sparked a revival of sorts, and he was nearly deported for practicing religion without a license. While Burke may be guilty of occasional exaggeration, comparisons of his concerts to religious revivals are commonplace.[22]

Whatever his convictions, Burke's very life has been a virtual study in the art of eclecticism. His pursuits have included the ministry, his recording career, the support of his twenty-one children, and the management of his chain of mortuaries.

The similarities between Mayfield's background and Burke's background are striking. Both were born and raised in the North—Mayfield in Chicago, Burke in Philadelphia. Both were the grandsons of female preachers who pastored churches. Both sang gospel as children. Whether Burke was born in 1935, 1936, or 1940, both he and Mayfield, who was born in 1942, were fairly close in age. The secular careers of both began in the 1950s and flourished in the early to mid-1960s.

An interesting contrast between the two is that Mayfield, while not formally ordained to preach, did so with great conviction in his secular hits. Compared to Burke, Mayfield's use of folk-preaching aesthetics is subdued, but the lyrics to his songs are laden with African-American religious significance. Burke, who *was* an ordained preacher, avoided sermonizing in the hits that brought him widespread popularity. At least until 1968, when he released "I Wish I Knew (How It Would Feel to Be Free)," Burke's best-known hits were void of social commentary. Yet, the aesthetics of the black preacher are as present in his secular work as they are in his ministry, which as of 1998 included spiritual oversight for the 168 churches within his bishopric.[23] Burke maintained a clear separation between his role as a spiritual leader and his identity as a secular entertainer perhaps because he identified more closely with that earlier generation of blacks who considered it inappropriate to fuse the two. This may be a reason to suspect that one of the earlier birth dates reported for Burke is the real one after all.

By the early 1970s, black secular music containing social commentary had evolved into the "message song," a genre associated with artists including Marvin Gaye, Stevie Wonder, and the Staple Singers. While message songs represented another variation on the preaching tradition of the black church, they tended to skirt around explicit proselytism for Christianity; instead, they preached a more generic, one-size-fits-all gospel of love, humanitarianism, and social and political responsibility. References to God or to Jesus in these message songs tend to occur sparingly, and, when they do, *God* is much broader in conception than fundamentalist Christianity would allow. The social message song was the bridge that the Staple Singers traversed in crossing over from gospel to secular performance. In an interview for *Goldmine,* Mavis Staples recalls the time when songwriter Bettye Crutcher tried to dissuade her from embellishing a song with religious expressions: "I didn't do the song. I *wouldn't* do it . . . what I wanted to say in the song, she [Bettye Crutcher] wanted me to say it differently. I told her I have to take the song and make it mine. I have to sing it the way I feel it. And then, it sounded kind of atheistic, 'cuz I think I wanted to say God or Jesus or something and she just wanted me to say *he*. She didn't want me to call the Lord's name. So she said, 'No Mavis, it's *he*.' So I said, 'Hey, Al Bell, you take this Bettye Crutcher [song], I can't sing the song. I'm sorry' and that was that."[24]

Although profit-conscious producers were leery about using the Lord's name, neither God nor Jesus disappeared completely from the social message song. This is perhaps due to the fact that the Staple Singers, Marvin Gaye, and Stevie Wonder were all inextricably rooted in the black church, and as the old adage goes, you can take the singer out of the church, but taking the church out of the singer meets with some difficulty.

The lengthy name of Marvin Gaye's childhood church is suggestive of the legalistic doctrine to which its members adhered: *The House of God, the Holy Church of the Living God, the Pillar and Ground of*

Marvin Gaye
(Author's collection)

the Truth, the House of Prayer for All People. In Gaye's church, members were required to keep the Saturday Sabbath, to observe Old Testament Jewish holidays, and women were required to wear white to worship services. Gaye's biographer David Ritz describes the music as typically Pentecostal. While music was indispensable to worship, church members were forbidden to indulge in secular music. Despite the edict denouncing secular music, Gaye's earliest foray into this forbidden arena was perhaps to spite his father, with whom he had a strained relationship. Gaye never abandoned the essential tenets of his childhood faith, however, and even publicly credited his father for contributing to his spiritual development.

The fusion of Gaye's secular artistry and his spiritual background is seen in *What's Going On,* released in 1971. The album was not only his personal *magnum opus,* but was also the seminal cadre of musical sermonettes for that period.[25] Ritz provides a thorough analysis of the tracks on *What's Going On* in a chapter fittingly titled "Sermon From the Studio." Ritz states that "according to his own testimony, he'd felt the calling as a small child" and that "proof of his ability to preach is found in *What's Going On.*"[26]

Of particular interest are the three cuts from the album that hit the Top Ten on the soul and pop charts in 1971: "What's Going On," "Mercy Mercy Me," and "Inner City Blues." The popularity of these songs not only underscores Gaye's artful exploitation of new recording technology, but also shows a successful challenge to Berry Gordy's cautious, cookie-cutter approach to manufacturing hits. Gaye claimed that "from Jump Street, Motown fought *What's Going On.*"[27] Gordy's sensitivity to mainstream preference was indeed legendary, and the activism in the album would certainly have given him reason for a panic attack or two. Nonetheless, the public demonstrated its readiness to hear Gaye preach about the evils of war in the title track; they were ready for Gaye's sermon on the sins of pollution, radiation, and overpopulation in "Mercy Mercy Me," and they appreciated his empathy with the disenfranchised urbanite in "Inner City Blues." Interestingly, of these three songs, only one contains a reference to God, a single mention of the Almighty that is more rhetorical than devotional. In "Inner City Blues," Gaye's discourse on inflation, the draft, and "trigger-happy policin'" includes the statement, "God knows where we're headin'." While Gaye's other songs reference God and Jesus directly, the fact that the three chart-toppers contain no such references may indicate that the social sermonizing was more palatable to the mainstream consumer than the more explicitly religious material on other tracks. Furthermore, by 1971, the average American had grown accustomed to the image of the black preacher as social activist, thanks to the canonization of Martin Luther King Jr. In *What's Going On,* Gaye was another black preacher, picking up where King had left off.

During the same year, the Staple Singers released their own unique brand of sermon in "Respect Yourself," a song that reached number two on the rhythm-and-blues charts and number twelve on the pop charts. It was the title cut of their album, which soared to nineteen on the pop charts. As the title suggests, "Respect Yourself" shakes a moralizing finger in the face of any and everyone unclear about the meaning of respect. Pop Staples renders the opening lines while playing a funky yet sobering lead guitar on this track, and, in so doing, he invokes the image of the guitar-playing, early twentieth-century blues preacher. He sings, "If you disrespect everybody that you run into / How'n the world do you think anybody's spos'ta respect you." Immediately, his posture is authoritative, paternalistic. There is no proselytizing for Christianity *per se* in the track, but Pop, nonetheless, calls for respect of the preacher in the lines that follow: "If you don't give a heck about the man with the Bible in his hand / Just get out the way and let the gentleman do his thing." Thanks to the instrumentals and Mavis Staples's gut-wrenching vocals, "Respect Yourself" is brazen soul music at its best. The song, however, falls squarely within the category of message songs that speak not just to blacks but to the world at large. This becomes clear in the lines of text addressed to the Ku Klux Klan ("take your sheet off your face boy, it's a brand new day!") and the environmental activists. To this last group, the Staples render advice that is both clever and classic: "Keep talkin' 'bout the president won't stop air pollution / put your hand on your mouth when you cough—that'll help the solution.") "Respect Yourself" preaches a pragmatic message of self-accountability and admonishes its listeners to look inward rather than outward for solutions to social ills.

Although quite young at the time, Stevie Wonder had some pretty potent sermonizing of his own to render in his album *Innervisions*. Released in 1973, several of its songs are penetrating reflections on religion, race, economics, and society. Although the songs are laden with conviction, the album itself does not seem to champion any one specific point of view, other than Wonder's personal frustration about a world gone bad and in desperate need of viable solutions. His particular concern is the plight of African Americans. Wonder tackles the issue of drugs on three of the tracks: "Too High," "Living for the City," and "Jesus Children of America." In "Living for the City," Wonder tells the hopeless story of many blacks who migrate from poverty in the South to urban decay in the North. Once considered the "Promised Land," the urban North, by the 1970s, was plagued with drugs and offered more peril than promise to young, disadvantaged African Americans. A unique feature of this track is its use of a dramatic interlude, which depicts the arrest of a naive newcomer to the city who unwittingly agrees to traffic drugs in order to make a quick five dollars. In "Jesus Children of America," Wonder speaks directly to the drug addict: "Tell me junkie, if you're able . . . are you happy when you stick a needle in your vein?"

The junkie is not the only one that Wonder questions in "Jesus Children of America." He also questions the Holy Roller: "Are you standing for everything you talk about?" It is clear in *Innervisions* that Stevie Wonder is struggling with religious tradition and equally clear that he has given serious thought to religious alternatives. "Higher Ground" is Wonder's testimony of reincarnation, as the text ("I'm so glad that he let me try it again / cause my last time on earth I lived a whole world of sin") makes clear. Although Wonder reminds the listener in "Jesus Children of America," that "Jesus died on the cross for you," he uses the same track to plug transcendental meditation: "Transcendental meditation speaks of inner preservation / transcendental meditation gives you peace of mind."

Wonder's ambivalence about Christianity in *Innervisions* may stem from his childhood experiences in the church. Jeffrey Peisch states that "one time, Mama Lulu even took Stevie to a faith healer, who put his hands in Stevie's eyes and chanted religious words." Stevie Wonder recounts this experience: "'Stevie,' the man would say, 'do you believe in God?' and I would say, 'Yes,' and he would press harder in my eyes and cry 'Heal!' Then he'd say 'Do you see that?' and I would reply, 'No' and he would say 'Then you don't believe in the Holy Spirit enough.' That experience could have made me bitter, but I don't want to see anyway."[28]

Another awkward moment between Stevie Wonder and the church occurred when he dabbled in secular music. Wonder recounts sing-

Stevie Wonder (Author's collection)

ing secular music on the porches in his neighborhood while growing up: "We used to get pretty big crowds of people playing on those porches. I remember this one time . . . this lady who was a member of our church, she was Sanctified Holiness, but she was still a member of our church, the Whitestone Baptist Church, and she came along and she said, 'Oh Steve, I'm ashamed of you for playing that worldly music out here. I'm so ashamed of you.' Ha, I really blew it boy. I'd been a junior deacon at the church and I used to sing solo at the services. But she went and she told them what I was doing and they told me to leave. And that's how I became a sinner."[29] Even though Wonder was stripped of his junior deaconship and excommunicated from the church, *Innervisions* conveys the pondering and the social sermonizing of a young man who is deeply invested in spiritual matters.

In his 1977 study of perceptions of the black preacher, H. Beecher Hicks Jr. cited Roberta Flack's recording of "Reverend Lee," a song which describes the sexual temptation of a black Baptist preacher:

> This is a song about a very big,
> strong, black southern Baptist minister
> who thinks that he has his program all together—
> until he runs up against a lady who shows him that he
> ain't got it together. His name is
> Reverend Doctor Lee
> Reverend Lee, he went to the water
> And he prayed to the Lord 'bout old Satan's daughter
> yeah, yeah
> It seems in a dream, child,
> While he lay sleeping,
> She climbed in his bed,
> Starts rubbin' and weepin'
> Ah, she was twistin' and turnin';
> She was beggin' and pleadin',
> Loving and burning,
> Panting and breathing.
> "Reverend Lee," she said, "Lord knows I love you, child,
> I would not even place God above you."

Reverend Lee, he lifted his arms high,
Said, "Heavenly Father, take me home to the sky."
He said, "Lord, please don't test me,
Not down where she touched me.
Oh, my mind is so hazy, Lord, my body so hungry."
God rolled the thunder
Then heard the lightnin'.
He seemed to be angry,
O sho' was fright'ning
Grew louder and louder,
Darkened conditions.
Just then, a voice said: "God cannot be petitioned."
Just then, the devil emerged from the water
And he said in a dry voice: "Your God will not bother."
Reverend Lee ran screaming from the water;
He was hotly pursued by old Satan's daughter.
Reverend Lee," she said, "Reverend Lee,
Oh, do it to me, Reverend Lee, do it to me."[30]

Twenty-six percent of those responding to Hicks's survey viewed the song as an accurate description of the black preacher's moral character.[31] Although 74 percent of the respondents felt differently, the stereotype of the sexually compulsive black preacher has persisted. Lyrics from the earliest blues recordings describe the preacher as a sexual opportunist, and numerous deacon caricature tunes from the mid-century years make light of the preacher's conquests of females in his flock. (See, in particular, my discussion of "The Deacon Moves In" from chapter 3.)

Interestingly, Hicks's study was conducted at a time when Teddy Pendergrass was at the height of his fame. In 1976, Pendergrass left Harold Melvin and the Blue Notes to pursue a solo career. His self-titled debut album was released in 1977 and went platinum. Four more million-selling albums followed. To countless women, Pendergrass was the consummate sex symbol, and his tunes "Close the Door," "Turn Off the Lights," and "Spend the Night" were blatant invitations to erotic fantasy. Even so, Pendergrass's command of the folk-preaching aesthetic is perhaps the most salient aspect of his artistry. The speech-song is represented prominently in virtually everything Pendergrass recorded in his solo career. This aspect of his performance, however, was more than just part of the show. The fact that Pendergrass claimed the call to preach authenticates his particular style. Like so many others, Pendergrass hails from the Holiness tradition, and, according to a 1989 article in *Ebony,* he was an ordained minister by the age of ten.[32] But in his autobiography, *Truly Blessed,* Pendergrass softens this claim: "so much was made of my early preaching that I'm afraid some people got the wrong impression. I addressed the congregation a time or two, but I was never a full-time, Bible-thumping boy preacher."[33]

Yet, Pendergrass describes hearing a voice and receiving the call to preach when he was ten years old:

> Jolted from sleep, I sat up in bed. Someone had called me. The deep male voice seemed at once strange yet familiar. I looked around: still night, still my room. . . . I slipped back under the covers and soon dropped off to sleep. "Teddy." There it was again! I sprang out of bed, hurried back to my mother, and asked her again if she had called me. Again she denied it and sent me back to bed. I lay down and it happened again. When I told Mom, a peaceful look came over her face, she rose from her bed, and we knelt together and prayed. "Something wonderful has occurred," she told me. "You have heard the voice of the Spirit and received your calling."[34]

He further states:

> Initially, both Mom and I took my calling to be one to preach in the traditional sense. However, in time I realized that was not my specific calling. Still, I had been called to minister—to acknowledge and to share with others my belief in and commitment to the existence and power of Jesus Christ—in some way. . . . With all my heart, I believe that in my singing, God gave me a precious gift, and that He has allowed me to be heard by millions all over the

world. Even in those times when it might appear to the
world that my public persona in some way contradicted
their conceptions of "faith," I never lost sight of the obliga-
tion the Lord bestowed upon me with the gift of my voice.
That is why, throughout my career, I made sure that along
with my secular music I included songs that brought a
message, that inspired listeners, that gave people hope,
from "Bad Luck" and "Wake Up Everybody" to "Somebody Told Me" to "Truly Blessed."[35]

Pendergrass's "Somebody Told Me" is one of the cuts on his 1977
debut album. The song is an inspired sermon complete with a call for
social reform, homage to Jesus Christ, a quotation from the Bible, a
testimony of personal faith, and a warning of final judgement. Several times following the line "Somebody told me to deliver this message," Pendergrass chimes in: "And I know you know who it is."
This line is significant because it is Pendergrass's appeal to the Christian consciousness tacitly assumed to be common to most African
Americans. The phenomenal success of the album may suggest that
the appeal did not fall on deaf ears. Most African Americans relate to
the concept of divine message and most would have known exactly
who had told Pendergrass to deliver it. Nonetheless, the critics were
confused when, during his debut solo performance at Carnegie Hall,
Pendergrass, wearing a white, sequined robe, sang "Somebody Told
Me" for his encore. Pendergrass states: "Not surprisingly, several
reviewers mentioned the seeming contradiction that would mark my
work forever: the mix of the sensual and the sacred. As the *New York
Times* put it: 'Mr. Pendergrass seems to want to have his cake and eat
his communion wafer too,' but it was intended as a compliment, not
as a put-down. It seemed that the only thing the critics didn't like was
the robe. Hey, you win some, you lose some."[36]
    Although Christianity has been the predominant religion of blacks
in America, non-Christian spirituality has been alive and well in the
African-American community since the time of slavery. Along with
Christianity, black slaves practiced various forms of conjuring. Conjuring, which came from the Yoruba of Africa, was a way to exert
control and influence, and it involved the use of incantations and

roots to either induce harm or ensure good luck. Conjurers also told fortunes and interpreted signs, natural phenomena believed to have prophetic significance. Many slaves also practiced the Muslim faith. Stacey Close gives this account of Bu Allah, an influential Muslim in the slave community: "Bu Allah was described as being an African of superior intelligence and character. Bu Allah reared his children in the Muslim faith. Three times a day, he would spread his sheepskin prayer rug to the East and pray to Allah. Bu Allah lived to be a very old man and when buried, his Koran and prayer rug were buried along with him."[37]

Disillusioned with what many considered to be the hypocrisy of Americanized Christianity, blacks have long considered alternative religions in their quest for spiritual fulfillment. Particularly in the 1960s, young African Americans considered religious alternatives that would address issues of racial identity and equality. As the traditional pulpit of the black church spawned its share of secular entertainers, other preaching voices emerged in secular music that represented a departure from tradition. Nowhere in black secular music does this departure from tradition become more salient in the 1970s than in funk.

Funk's representative artists include George Clinton's Parliament-Funkadelic, Kool and the Gang, the Ohio Players, Earth, Wind, and Fire, Graham Central Station, Bootsy's Rubber Band, the Bar-kays, and the Commodores. As a style of music, funk emphasizes group singing, an imaginative, often percussive bass line, a prominent horn section, and lyrics that direct its participants to party with reckless abandon. It is very difficult, however, to describe funk in strictly musical terms. As salient as the music itself is funk's philosophy. During the 1960s, many black Americans rejected racial assimilation and looked instead to their own cultural roots for meaning and identity. Part of this process involved exchanging the traditional black church heritage for an African religious perspective. "Funk," says Rickey Vincent, "is deeply rooted in African cosmology—the idea that people are created in harmony with the rhythms of nature and that free expression is tantamount to spiritual and mental health."[38] Funk's emphasis on oneness and sexual, physical, and mental liberation contrasts greatly with the good-versus-evil dichotomy of Western Christian thought and presents a challenge to traditional notions of salvation and redemption.

In funk jargon, "the rhythm of the one" is an important expression, one that Vincent relates to the spiritual trance state associated with West-African ritualistic dancing. As in African ritual, the rhythms in funk encourage participants to dance, thereby creating and intensifying a collective *pulse*. Vincent states that "when George Clinton is heard chanting on stage 'On the one, everybody on the one,' he isn't trying to get the band on the beat (they are already there), he is savoring the rhythmic lock that has brought the entire house together, as one." Black identity and black pride are central to the oneness and liberation emphasized in funk.[39]

The musical exploration of alternatives to Christianity did not originate with the 1970s funk phenomenon. The quest of Herman Blount, later known as Sun Ra, had a profound effect on the spiritual dimension of funk, an effect that is woefully understated in Rickey Vincent's book. In citing the influence of Sun Ra upon Parliament-Funkadelic, Earth, Wind, and Fire, and other funk bands, Vincent devotes a single paragraph to Sun Ra, crediting him for originating the space traveler imagery so salient in funk.[40] The spiritual link between Sun Ra and funk entails more than the space traveler imagery, and an understanding of funk's philosophical dimension begins with a discussion of Sun Ra's unique approach to religion. Herman Blount's musicianship was informed by the spiritual musing he had indulged in from the time he was a child. While he claimed to have not been born (one of several bizarre claims), his biographer, John Szwed, notes his birth on May 22, 1914, to a woman fascinated with Afrocentric magic. He was named after Black Herman, "the most famous of many early twentieth-century Afrocentric magicians." Black Herman was part Jew, part Black nationalist, and reportedly raised the dead during his shows. Charlatan or not, Black Herman was celebrated by the black community, perhaps because he gave them a sense of empowerment.[41]

By the time he was in the first grade, Herman Blount's grandmother and great aunt had seen to his enrollment in the Baptist church. Even then, exposure to Christianity sparked questions that sent him on a spiritual search for the better part of his life. While still a youngster, he read voraciously on religion, world history, psychic phenomena, the occult, and the Bible. By World War II, Blount had aligned himself with the Seventh-Day Adventists and avoided military service by becoming a religious objector. However, since he was not a member of any church, the judge who heard his case was less than convinced and sentenced him to jail pending further disposal of his case. Afterward, a brief assignment to a military camp ended when Blount, found to be physically unfit, mentally unstable, and possessed of "a psychopathic personality," was released.[42]

In his biography of Sun Ra, Szwed describes a man whose passionate, somewhat obsessive quest for spiritual enlightenment clearly became the impetus behind virtually every noteworthy thing he did. As he developed musically, Blount immersed himself in Egyptology. He devoured the writings of John G. Jackson, Godfrey Higgins, Grafton Elliot Smith, Gerald Massey, George G.M. James, and others who seemed to provide answers to his probing questions about deity, the origin of civilization, and the role of black people. Despite his bizarre claims of having no birth date and of being reared by the Creator himself, Blount's spiritual quest left him with a profound analytic insight, not to mention incredibly well read. By the mid-1950s, Blount had attracted a small following which took his philosophies seriously enough to organize their own research on the Bible, astrology, music, and science. A major focus of this undertaking was to locate proof of the black man's primacy in world history, proof that could not be found in conventional Christianity. This study group eventually became Ihnfinity, Inc.

It was in 1952 that Herman Blount legally became Sun Ra, the name-change itself derived from the occult. While he wrote for several rhythm-and-blues groups (including the Moonglows, the Spaniels, and the El-Dorados) and while he played piano for a gospel label in the late 1950s, Sun Ra's vision for his music transcended entertainment. He was a believer, for example, in the healing power of music. As evidence, he frequently cited the story of his performance at a Chicago mental hospital during which he was able to elicit a response from a woman who had not moved or spoken in years.[43]

Sun Ra's spirituality also included a deep interest in outer space, a theme common to both Egyptology and Islam. Islam taught that at the appointed time, the end of the world would be brought about by means of the Mother Ship, a huge, invisible aircraft constructed by ancient black scientists that would be used to exterminate the enemies of Allah. In homage to the solar boat, or "ark" of the Egyptian god Ra, Sun Ra changed the name of his band to the Arkestra. In fact, Sun Ra frequently changed the name of his band to monikers alluding, in various ways, to outer space, the galaxy, or cosmic reality. Some of the names of his band included Cosmic Space Jazz Group, Solar-Hieroglyphics Arkestra, Intergalactic Research Arkestra, Astro-Solar Arkestra, and many others. Sun Ra's interest in outer space also became evident in his selection of colors and costumes for his band. Inspired by his reading of color associations among the Egyptians, Greeks, and Tibetans, Sun Ra used color to make decisions about a variety of things, from food to room assignments for his musicians. Sun Ra eventually adapted a space motif for the band's costume designs. He described his motivation as follows: "We started [wearing space costumes] back in Chicago. In those days, I tried to make the black people, the so-called Negroes, conscious of the fact that they live in a changing world. . . . We're like space warriors. Music can be used as a weapon, as energy. The right note or chord can transport you into space using music and energy flow. And the listeners can travel along with you."[44]

By the 1960s, Sun Ra's concerts had evolved into techno-spirit-cosmic spectacles. He used his music to proselytize for his rather complex belief system drawn together from a variety of sources. Speaking of his compositions, Ra states that "the real aim of this music is to coordinate the minds of people into an intelligent reach for a better world, and an intelligent approach to the living future."[45] The religious aura of Ra's concerts was hardly lost on those who attended them, and his use of chants and audience participation closely approximated an effort to bring about some type of cosmic spirit possession. Szwed writes that "the atmosphere created in the latter part of the performance seemed churchlike, calling up to some people memories of Baptist pageants, and Sunday services, sermons, and hymns, the interplay of preacher, choirs, and congregation which leads to ecstasy."[46]

Many of Sun Ra's chants were derived directly from the hymns and spirituals of the black church. In particular, Ra enjoyed chants based upon "Swing Low, Sweet Chariot," "This World Is Not My Home," and other sacred songs that evoked "a world in which people fly all over heaven, ride chariots in the sky, and encouraged his audiences to prepare to depart with him to outer space." Szwed notes further that "these chants were usually done with the Arkestra shuffling, making little jumps, and clapping in a counter-clockwise circle as in the old Negro shouts."[47] Thus, like the black preachers of Christian tradition, Sun Ra was concerned with moving his "congregation" from *here* to *there,* from the physical circumstances of the present to a higher level of consciousness.

For Sun Ra, jazz was little more than a means for preaching his unique gospel of Egyptology, astrology, Islam, revised Christianity, and ancient mysticism. A summary of his religious agenda can be found in the 1974 articles of incorporation for Ihnfinity, which describe its purpose as follows:

> To perform spiritual-cosmic-intergalactic-infinity research works relative to worlds-dimensions-planes in galaxies and universes beyond the present now known used imagination of mankind, beyond the intergalactic central sun and works relative to spiritual and spiritual advancement of our presently known world. To awaken the spiritual conscious of mankind putting him back in contact with his "Creator." To make mankind aware that there are superior beings (Gods) on other planets in other galaxies. To make mankind aware that the "Creator" (God) is here now and that he is also present in other world-galaxies. To help stamp out (destroy) ignorance destroying its major purpose changing ignorance to constructive creative progress.[48]

The link between Sun Ra and funk groups of the 1970s is clear. Sun Ra's unique spiritual potpourri surfaced in the costumes, stage props, and performance antics of groups like Earth, Wind, and Fire, Bootsy's Rubber Band, and Parliament-Funkadelic. In a September 1977 review of the Madison Square Garden "P-Funk Earth Tour" concert featuring Parliament-Funkadelic and Bootsy's Rubber Band, *New York Times* writer John Rockwell observed that "the dramatic arrival and departure of the Mothership flying saucer [was] properly placed toward the end" of the concert. He remarks further about P-Funk's first-rate instrumentalists, and then states: "Add to that Mr. Clinton's assortment of audience-participation chants (nearly all of them unprintable here) and the loving willingness of black audiences to so participate and you have an almost unstoppable combination. Sometime, the audience chant-alongs reached a fervor that approached mass choral singing. And when everyone dropped to a hushed croon on the words, 'Swing low, sweet chariot, let me ride,' over and over again before the saucer 'landed,' the music took on an almost mystical significance." He continues: "P-Funk is basically built for entertainment, not social message-sending like so many more self-consciously important black bands. But Mr. Clinton gets his message across in his own way."[49]

Of the stage props in the concert, the Mothership is the centerpiece, a symbol of Islam, of Afrocentricity, and, most important, of escape. As do the Negro spirituals, which reference chariots, ships, and trains, the Mothership of Funk represents the creation of alternative place, transport from *here* to *there*. Clinton facilitates this journey as he combines the imagery of the Mothership with the sound of a familiar strain from the black-American Christian church, "Swing low, sweet chariot." As do preachers of the conventional black pulpit, Clinton leads his audience in the creation of an aura that the reviewer not only calls "mystical," but also recognizes as part of Clinton's "message."

Another review, this time of Earth, Wind, and Fire's November 1977 Madison Square Garden concert, cites a similar air of mysticism. Robert Palmer of the *New York Times* writes:

> Men in spacesuits, their features hidden behind tinted glass
> visors, appear on the stage toward the end of Earth, Wind
> and Fire's new show, which was at Madison Square Garden
> on Thursday and Friday. They supervise the lowering of a
> pyramid-shaped space craft onto a raised platform and one
> by one the members of the band disappear into it. The thing

takes off, hoisted smoothly up into the air, and then there is
a puff of smoke and it bursts apart. It is empty. The men in
the space suits turn to face the audience and remove their
helmets. They are the same musicians who disappeared
into the pyramid moments before.

He continues:

This superior bit of parlor magic on a grand scale is just the
sort of thing that makes Earth, Wind and Fire special. It is
flashy, and the band is certainly that, with its brilliantly
colored costumes, energetic showmanship, and espousal of
various aspects of mysticism. But it is also magic, or
illusion, to give it its proper name, of the very best kind
because it stretches the imaginations and conceptual
boundaries of its viewers.[50]

Sun Ra's proselytizing seems to have found a following in the funk
groups that incorporated heavy doses of Egyptology, magic, outer
space, audience chanting, and twisted fragments of traditional Christianity into their acts.

Although religion figured prominently into funk (as Vincent's
detailed discussion shows), the principal architects of the music had
varied perceptions about their own roles as religious leaders. George
Clinton laid no serious claims to religious leadership. He was attracted to the philosophy of the Process Church of Final Judgment,
an obscure religious cult that called for acceptance of the negative as
a prerequisite to appreciating the positive. In the liner notes of both
his *Maggot Brain* album of 1971 and *America Eats Its Young,* which
soon followed, Clinton paid tribute to the Process Church. Although
Clinton's inadvertent proselytizing sparked a religious fervor of sorts,
he viewed himself more as an entertainer than as a preacher or prophet.

By contrast, Maurice White of Earth, Wind, and Fire saw himself
as a religious leader with a divine mandate. White's religious background, like Sun Ra's, was rather eclectic. He was reared in the Baptist Holiness Church of Memphis, Tennessee, but embraced Buddhism
while touring in Japan with Ramsey Lewis. Upon returning to Los

Angeles, White founded Earth, Wind, and Fire in 1970, naming the group for his astrological elements. White forbade his band members to indulge in smoking, in drinking, and in most meat. Before each concert, White required twenty minutes of meditation in a prayer circle.

In various interviews throughout the 1970s, White announced his religious agenda. In the November 8, 1976, issue of *People* magazine, he states that "this band has a very positive effect on people. . . . I feel we were elected to this by a higher force."[51] In a 1979 article for *High Fidelity,* he provides a thorough explanation of his mission:

> We feel that we are being used as a tool to say certain
> things. . . . Most black people walking around in the streets
> are very unhappy, very depressed. I truly feel myself that
> love is the better way, that when you can get inside and
> reacquaint yourself with yourself, you can make yourself a
> better life. I try to make a better way for them so they can
> face each day with a positive attitude. . . . Because we are
> living in this jive society, we tend to relate to the beautiful
> things—like the universe—in a very negative manner. So in
> the group we draw all of our forces from the universe, and
> from the Creator, and from the sky. Meditation is one way,
> though there's other ways too. . . . The group is very
> heavily into Egyptology. We felt that there were many
> secrets from that era that have never been totally worked
> out. Also that some of our spirituality and ideas relate to
> Egyptology. . . . Our total concept is to create an illusionary
> effect in our public's mind. We're trying to reacquaint them
> with the Egyptian civilization so they can search and find
> out new things about themselves.[52]

In a March 1979 article on Earth, Wind, and Fire for *Melody Maker,* Vivien Goldman writes that "Maurice White has expressed over and over again in interviews that they have a message of love to preach to the world."[53]

Maurice White's missionary zeal is pronounced in Earth, Wind, and Fire's most popular output of the 1970s. In the mid-1970s, much of the commercial music industry was being swept up in the tidal wave of disco, and the group's "Boogie Wonderland," recorded in 1979 with the Emotions, was its principal, somewhat after-the-fact contribution to that particular genre. Earlier in the decade, they had already become known for songs that were thoughtful, provocative, motivational, and inspirational. White takes his calling seriously in numerous songs written to point the listener in a positive spiritual direction. Words like *love, peace,* and *happiness* run the risk of being cliché and hypersimplistic, but they really do summarize White's musical sermons. In hit after hit, Earth, Wind, and Fire tell their audiences to be their best, share with others, and look inward to find love, peace, and happiness. In "Shining Star," the group sings a message of affirmation: "You're a shining star, no matter who you are." "Sing a Song" touts music as emotional remedy, and "In the Stone" tells where real strength, love, and peace reside: "In the stone you'll find the meaning . . . the greatest love . . . is written in the stone," which, of course, is a metaphor for somewhere deep inside your heart.

The earlier social sermons of Marvin Gaye and Stevie Wonder address the problems of a society plagued with particular social, political, economic, and environmental ills. Earth, Wind, and Fire's music, by contrast, directs the listener to look inside for a more personal salvation. Lines like "you will find peace of mind if you look way down in your heart and soul" from "That's the Way of the World" are typical homiletic fare in the repertoire of Earth, Wind, and Fire. Their brand of evangelism is also universal in its appeal, as opposed to race or culture specific. Maurice White's sermons transcend the boundaries of black America and its unique circumstance. His oft-repeated directive to look inside for peace, love, and happiness is meant for all people listening everywhere.

His global perspective notwithstanding, White saved a place in his output for black church tradition. The group's 1974 album, *Open Our Eyes,* includes the 1958 gospel song by the same name. "Open Our Eyes," which is a prayer for peace and faith, avoids the use of idiosyncratic jargon, or the words *God, Jesus,* or *Christ.* Instead, the prayer is addressed to *Father, Master,* and *Lord.* When released in 1974, Earth, Wind, and Fire's rendition of the song would have conjured familiar images of the traditional black church for many African Americans. Its praise of universal virtues, however, is in keeping with White's more global inspirational agenda.

Although White sought to enlighten the world with peace, hope, and love, there could be little question about where his more specific religious sympathies lay. Earth, Wind, and Fire was able to attract a mainstream audience because the group obeyed the cardinal rule of crossing over: Avoid iconoclasm. Yet, there are moments where White's religious preferences surface in the music with as much candor as they do in the many interviews he has given over the course of his career. One example is in "All About Love," which was released on the 1975 *That's the Way of the World* album. In this song, a spoken interlude announces the group's religious philosophy. A generic essay on love suddenly turns to proselytizing when the speaker, presumably White, explains: "We study all kinds of cults, sciences, astrology, mysticism, world religion, and so forth . . . coming from a hip place, all these things help because they give you an insight into your inner self." The sermonette then segues into a discussion on the virtues of self-love. The sedative musical accompaniment never misses a beat as this weighty exhortation unfolds.

Maurice White's call to preach peace, hope, and love to the world and his effort to attain the same for himself and his group through a global religious consciousness makes a powerful statement about African Americans in the 1970s. In earlier times, blues preachers, living in a segregated, often hostile America, shaped their "sermons" according to the boundaries of their racial identity and the cultural specificity of their religious roots. With the mainstreaming of African Americans by the 1970s, those cultural boundaries broaden to include more than just blacks and more than just Christianity. Groups like Earth, Wind, and Fire preach sermons in their secular music reflective of this expanded social and religious awareness.

By the 1970s, black secular music had become as much a venue for preaching as the traditional pulpit of the black church. Just as the religious expectations of blacks had come to place heavy emphasis on social and political concerns, the secular dimension of black culture had also evolved to include the preaching voices once confined to the black church. In style, substance, form, and function, preaching by the 1970s was a legitimate and commonplace component of black secular music. Its legitimacy during this period contrasts with the earlier conservatism that marginalized the blues preacher for delivering sermons beyond the sanctuary.

2pac (Author's collection)

Postlude

GOD AND GANGSTA RAP

The Theosophy of Tupac Shakur

When I handed her my check for the purchase of a Tupac Shakur compilation CD, the cashier seemed slightly aghast that someone my age could be interested in gangsta rap. Indeed, this was my first such purchase. I'd spent a good twenty minutes circling the isles of alphabetized recordings in the shop before I realized that the first syllable of the artist's name was represented by the number *2* and not by the letters *TU*. The CD cover showed a close-up of Tupac, a "Parental Advisory" label warning of explicit content, and the logo of Death Row Records, this last item alone speaking volumes to me. Nonetheless, I left the shop with my very own Tupac Shakur recording in hand, a new initiate into that class of consumers whose dollars transform the obscene into the commonplace.

My students led me to Tupac. Every year, I teach a course in African-American music which, for the students, culminates in a final paper. After our study of musical genres spanning West Africa to contemporary trends, I require the students to write a paper on any topic of their choice related to black music. In 1996, I received my first truckload of papers on Tupac Shakur. Students representing a variety of racial, ethnic, and economic backgrounds had chosen to memorialize the recently slain artist in papers that I perceived to be more heartfelt than purely academic. Unlike the students who had written on Scott Joplin and Marian Anderson, the students who wrote papers on Tupac were on a mission to educate me with pictures, lyrics, newspaper clippings, CD jackets, and anything else they could

149

get their hands on to show what this man meant to them. In the years that followed, students continued to write about Tupac, and as of the Spring of 2001 his name had still not completely disappeared from our discussions of contemporary black music.

As this book neared its final form, it was my desire to "shift gears," as it were, and offer some personal reflections on the meaning of religion in black popular music from a contemporary perspective. The older I get, the more my students remind me that what I consider contemporary is actually old school. Consequently, I become increasingly dependent upon their perspectives as I attempt to interpret current trends and sift through the commercialism to locate the truly significant. Several years of genuinely heartfelt student papers convince me that Tupac Shakur has achieved enough iconicity to serve as the focus of these personal reflections.

In my teaching, I had always taken a safe, academic approach to the treatment of rap music—particularly of gangsta rap. From behind my professor's podium, I conveyed the sociocultural background of the music, the important architects of the genre, the significant record labels, noteworthy writings, stylistic evolution, and so forth and so on. In deference to my colleagues, who could hear my lectures through very thin walls, I chose to play musical examples that steered clear of controversy. "Rapper's Delight" was a regular feature of my introductory lecture on rap, but hard-core material never made its way into my playlist. I felt that a perfectly well-rounded lecture on rap could take place in my classroom without reference to *bitches, whores,* and *muthafuckas.*

I reserve the right to be repulsed by the repulsive. Nonetheless, I have come to realize that my caution in the classroom was, to some extent, informed by my self-righteous condescension. While *fuck, pussy,* and *bitch* are not my favorite words, they are, after all, *only words,* and I allowed them to block me from the poet's deeper meaning.

Herein lies the issue: Throughout my study of religion in black popular music, I have given particular attention to lyrics. I have shown how the blues poet's use of biblical imagery and metaphor represents a link to a God-centered, antebellum past. At the same time, I have shown how blues poetry offers scathing critiques of conservative church life, evidence of the younger generation's quest for more meaningful and relevant religiosity. I have shown how, during the mid-century years, black secular song parodied and satirized black religion, a practice that sprang from the minstrel tradition, the jokelore tradition of black culture, and black America's growing tendency for self-appraisal in light of Euro-American norms. I have discussed the subjugation of religious themes in the lyrics of black secular record-ings during the 1950s crossover phase of black music, and the nature of the preacher persona in the political and inspirational message songs of the post–Civil Rights era. These findings notwithstanding, my argument—that secular song portrays black religious conscious-ness—falls short unless I am willing to probe for that consciousness in lyrics that make me uncomfortable. Rap, after all, *is* lyrics. It is message, scantily clad, front and center.

As this postlude is my place for personal reflection, I will not duplicate the more comprehensive treatments of rap presented with such elegance in works by Tricia Rose, Nelson George, and others. I make no attempt here to critically assess the music from a scholarly vantage point. Instead, I use this place to assume more of a layman's stance and to describe how I experienced and understood the music when I gave my undivided attention to Tupac Shakur.

On a purely sensory level, I was drawn into the rhythm of the poetry, into the percussiveness of the consonants, into the inflections of the vowels, into the emotion of the delivery, and into the absolute realization that this poet was determined to make me know his story. Everything beyond the lyrics was embellishment—the sampling, the technology, the sound effects. The music—at once beautiful, bland, haunting, dissonant, and repetitive—paled in comparison to the col-orful narratives that yanked me from my comfort zone.

Tupac was born in 1971, the same year that Marvin Gaye re-leased *What's Going On,* the same year that the Staples released "Re-spect Yourself," the same year that Melvin Van Peeples released the first of the blaxploitation films, *Sweet Sweetback's Baadasssss Song.*[1] As if his birth year were strategically coordinated with these events, his short life was an amalgam of the acutely tragic condition of being black, young, male, urban, and "at risk" late in the twentieth century. Tupac's music sits on the extreme end of the same continuum where we find other social message songs, from Billie Holiday's riveting rendition of "Strange Fruit" in 1939 to Marvin Gaye's "Inner City Blues" of 1971. In his "Keep Ya Head Up," released in 1993, Tupac cites Marvin Gaye's influence upon his life: "I remember Marvin Gaye used to sing to me / he had me feelin' like black was the thing to be / suddenly the ghetto didn't seem so tough / though we had it rough / we always had enough." Sadly, both Gaye and Shakur died violently, in bizarre fulfillment of the unrest and despair conveyed in their music. We might also note that the elder Gaye and the younger Tupac also illustrate a disturbing trend, one backed by oft-reported sociological data. Gaye's untimely death at forty-five years of age (actually, just one day shy of his forty-fifth birthday) preceded by twelve years Tupac's untimely death at twenty-five years of age. Black men dying younger, dying in greater numbers.

Some might argue that the parallels between Gaye and Shakur stop here, for Gaye, unlike Shakur, was drenched in a religious upbringing that permeated both his secular output and persona. His drug problems and embittered relationship with his father notwithstanding, Gaye's God-consciousness was salient, emphatic, unquestioned. Few might have the same perception of Tupac, the thug.[2] Even so, I locate deep religious sentiment in the music of Tupac: God, death, redemption, and the afterlife are themes that surface repeatedly in his music.

While he lived, Tupac's religious consciousness was certainly upstaged by the other shaping forces of his truncated life. The son of Black Panther Afeni Shakur, Tupac was born a month after his mother's release from the Women's House of Detention in Greenwich Village. She, along with others, had been convicted of conspiracy to bomb several sites in New York. Tupac's biological father was absent for most of his life, and his upbringing was plagued by poverty, transience, occasional homelessness, and drugs. Albeit dismal, the tapestry of his life bore salient threads of the church. Afeni Shakur had lived her own drama of revolutionary involvement, prison time, drug addiction, and either in spite of this or because of this she joined the church in 1981 when Tupac was ten years old. She affiliated with the House of the Lord Church in Brooklyn, and its pastor, the Reverend Herbert Daughtry, was the same one who would eulogize Tupac fifteen years later. Armond White's biography of Tupac suggests that Daughtry's role in Tupac's life was more than ceremonial. Reverend Daughtry was a regular visitor to New York's Rikers Island Penitentiary when Tupac served time there for sexual assault in 1995. Reverend Daughtry listened when Tupac explained his music and even offered feedback on some of the songs when asked. Reverend Daughtry's compassionate regard for Tupac no doubt influenced the rapper's concept of God and also solidified his sense of personal faith.[3]

Daughtry's influence upon Tupac may have also been particularly significant in light of the rapper's desperate desire for male affirmation. In "Dear Mama," a song so powerful it moved me to tears, Tupac describes with riveting clarity how his father's absence affected his life. He explains his attraction to the older thugs in his neighborhood by describing the void that these young men filled in his own life: "Even though they sold drugs / they showed a young brother love." Unfortunately, the drug dealers had a greater presence in Tupac's life than did Reverend Daughtry. Daughtry, however, may deserve some credit for the fact that there seems to be no outright blasphemy (at least, none that I could find) in Tupac's music. Its explicit and sometimes disturbing content notwithstanding, Tupac's references to God are generally reverent and indicative of a genuine faith.

While Reverend Daughtry certainly seems to have influenced his spirituality in a positive way, Tupac's religious questions may have been brewing long before Afeni took him to church. In his songs, Tupac claims to have witnessed the deaths of his peers since childhood. Certainly, a significant portion of his artistic output was written to memorialize his dead peers. Childhood exposure to violent death undoubtedly brought Tupac into premature contact with the question of mortality, the meaning of his own existence, its purpose and its fragility. His raps are full of questions and conclusions about death, some of the most chilling of which are collected in several albums released posthumously.

Tupac wrote "God Bless the Dead" in homage to his peers whose deaths preceded his own. What strikes me about this posthumous release (Interscope Records, 1998) is that despite the troubling nature of Tupac's lifestyle, he emerges in these lyrics as a man of faith—a man who clearly believes in God, prays to God, and envisions an afterlife. His peers fall victim to an irrational and violent world, yet Tupac's emotional proximity to God is such that he asks, "Why did You have to take a good one . . . ?" He asks the same question ("Tell me Lord, why You take big Cato?) in "How Long Will They Mourn Me?" which was released in 1994 and written in honor of another fallen friend. This question is all the more striking in its revelation of Tupac's two-tiered understanding of how the world works. On one level, Tupac clearly understands that violence is to blame for the deaths of his young peers. On a deeper, more sublime level, the very question indicates Tupac's belief that behind all of the chaos and craziness, God represents a higher order of things, a logic behind that which is illogical in this world. To ask the question, "Why did you have to take a good one . . . ?" is proof of Tupac's belief that God holds the answer. Whether an answer is granted, of course, is always God's prerogative.

In "God Bless the Dead," Tupac offers a hint of his view of the afterlife. He begins by addressing rival rapper Biggie Small (Christopher Wallace), who was connected to Tupac's 1996 murder, and who, himself, was gunned down on March 9, 1997. He says, "Rest in peace to my muthafuckin' Biggie Smalls [*sic*]. . . . Don't worry if you see God first / tell Him shit got worse / I ain't mad—I know you representin' the crew / I can picture you in heaven with a blunt and a brew." For me, the significance of this statement lies not in its obvious prophetic sensibility (both Tupac and Biggie Small were dead before the song's release), nor in Tupac's particular concept of a heaven flowing with drugs and alcohol. What strikes me here is Tupac's belief that there is a heaven at all, his belief that there is recourse, redemption, continuation. Belief in heaven seems to solve for him the problem of a hostile and degenerate world. In fact, "Fuck the world" is a favorite refrain of Tupac's, and he repeats it in this and other songs. That Tupac can picture someone in heaven "with a blunt and a brew" is unremarkable, since most of us who envision heaven incorporate our favorite earthly things into that vision. For some of us, heaven is not just pearly gates and streets of gold, but it is also a place where we eat our favorite foods, reconnect with those gone on before, and enjoy utter tranquility, however we conceptualize this state of mind. In "God Bless the Dead," as well as in other raps, Tupac's lyrics are autobiographical. He goes into great detail about his upbringing in the ghetto, his childhood exposure to violence and decay, his restless and suffocating environment, and his resultant paranoia. Against this troubling backdrop, it's no wonder that "a blunt and a brew" would symbolize the calmer moments of Tupac's earthly existence, and no wonder that these symbols of peace became part of his concept of heaven.

Tupac collaborated with several other artists to write "Hail Mary," which was released in November 1996, just weeks after his death. "Hail Mary" is the nightmarish poetry of a young man driven mad by the violent hopelessness of his existence. While "God Bless the Dead" offered a glimpse of postmortem, heavenly contentment, "Hail Mary" portrays Tupac's nervous anticipation of death. Early in the rap, we hear the rapper say "And God said He should send His one begotten Son to lead the wild into the ways of the man. . . . Follow me. . . . Eat my flesh, flesh of my flesh." These lines convey a religious awareness superimposed with the kind of confusion that insanity engenders. In these lines, Tupac references Christ as God's "one begotten Son." In addition, the lines "Follow me" and "Eat my flesh" are excerpted from the Gospels, where Christ instructs His disciples to follow Him, and, later, instructs them to eat His flesh as represented in the bread of the Last Supper before the crucifixion. Tupac's subtle, yet clever connection of Christ's death to his own extends a poetic tradition that was born during the antebellum era. Black slaves always likened their suffering to that of Biblical figures, as numerous Negro spirituals illustrate. Daniel in the lion's den, Jonah in the whale, and Jesus on the cross were recurrent themes in the spirituals, and these images of suffering served as a link between the Christian faith and the slaves' reality. I would say the same about Tupac and "Hail Mary." References to Christ in this rap are salient because the rapper connects Christ's suffering to his own.

Tupac's treatment of religion in his music parallels that of the early twentieth-century blues poets. Blues lyrics of the 1920s, 1930s, and 1940s tend to contain highly descriptive, autobiographical material full of explanations about the nature of, and reasons for, the poet's emotional state. Frequently, God, the Devil, or both somehow figure into those explanations. The overwhelming sense of impending doom that I hear in Tupac's music reminds me of the same type of paranoia that comes through in the music of Robert Johnson. As did Johnson in "Me and the Devil Blues," Tupac almost seems to revel in chilling predictions of his own demise. Convinced that he would die young, Tupac used his music to face fate head-on, perhaps as a way to deal with his fear.

While death may have been a particular obsession of Tupac's, he produced many songs on lighter subjects. Two of my favorites are "Keep Ya Head Up," a compassionate and inspirational tribute to women, and "Unconditional Love," in which he describes friend-ship, devotion, and commitment. A few lines in "Unconditional Love" are particularly striking to me because they convey Tupac's religious sensibility on several levels. He says: "How many caskets can we witness / Before we see it's hard to live this life without God / so we must ask forgiveness." In many other songs, Tupac explains his tor-mented lifestyle in terms of his disenfranchisement while growing up and his negative environment. In these lines, however, he offers a different point of view: Violence and death are the result of living life apart from God. Like the blues artists of earlier generations, Tupac's religious self-assessment included both an acknowledgment of his distance from God coupled with a strong belief in God's redemptive power. At the moment that he says "we must ask forgiveness," Tupac assumes the role of the preacher. From his own fallen state, he points to a better way. Like other preachers who sermonized from secular pulpits, Tupac proselytizes in these lines, not from a place of judg-mental condescension but rather from a place of complete empathy with those who share his particular view of the world.

Tupac's experiences afforded him the credentials to preach about the social decay that gave rise to his tragic and famous persona. While Marvin Gaye could sing about war, he had never actually been on a battlefield, on the front line, in the direct line of fire. Tupac, on the other hand, had been there. His descriptions of ghetto life are so dis-armingly graphic because they are often his accounts of situations he knew of first hand. I don't know of any factual basis for "Brenda's Got a Baby," but Tupac's in-your-face narrative about the repercussions of a twelve-year-old's pregnancy smacks of authenticity. Perhaps "Brenda" was someone that Tupac knew from the ghetto, or perhaps she is the composite of many women from Tupac's neighborhood who lived different facets of this catastrophic tale. Either way, "Brenda's Got a Baby" is a heart-pricking parable that Tupac preaches, not for shock value, but in order to, as he says, "show you how it affects our whole community." In the rap, Brenda is impregnated at twelve years old by a cousin who molests her. She hides her pregnancy from her family and gives birth on the bathroom floor. She attempts to dispose of the baby in a trash heap, but returns to rescue him after hearing his cries. Unable to support the new life, Brenda's family releases her to the streets where she is forced to make her own way. Too poor to pay a babysitter, Brenda is unable to keep a job, so "She tried to sell crack, but end up getting robbed." Her only recourse is to sell herself, and through prostitution she is able to pay the rent and feed her child. In one fell swoop, "Brenda's Got a Baby" explains one of the ugliest sources of urban decay.

I am convinced that the brutal honesty of "Brenda's Got a Baby" is a response to the cultural climate of Tupac's coming of age. Tupac would have been a teenager during the mid-1980s, a period when Americans of all demographic makeups nurtured an obsession with *The Cosby Show*. While this sitcom portrayed African Americans in gloriously positive roles, its idyllic picture of life was too perfect for even the most well-adjusted and privileged of white families to emulate. Not only did the Cosby's present a picture of a two-parent black family living in a brownstone, but the parents in the family each worked full-time in high-paying professions while, at the same time, managing to rear, not one, but five intelligent, well-balanced children in a beautifully decorated home that was perpetually tidy, warm, and inviting. Although I was a *Cosby Show* devotee myself in the 1980s, I am wondering now whether that fantasy world actually did a major disservice to the millions of African Americans living in a reality light years apart from the Huxtables. While Clair and Cliff enjoyed meaningful interaction with their five well-fed children, Tupac and Afeni Shakur were struggling to exist as a single-parent family, struggling to pay the rent, struggling to eat. The closest approximation of a Cliff Huxtable in Tupac's life was the drug dealer who affirmed him and showed him the ropes of ghetto survival. The potency of "Brenda's Got a Baby" and the power of Tupac's music in general may indeed come from his need to scream the truth of his existence over the noise of a fictitious, yet pervasive sitcom culture.

It is perhaps fitting that Tupac's "Unconditional Love" contains another example of the rapper's identification with the suffering Christ: "Ask Mama why God deserved to die / witness the tears falling free from my eyes before she could reply." To me, the deep sentiment conveyed in these lines underscores the importance that African Americans have always placed upon God's ability to empathize with their plight. A much more direct expression of the rapper's faith in the suffering Christ is his "Black Jesuz," a rap done in collaboration with the group Outlawz. "Black Jesuz" explains the rapper's religious position with depth and clarity, and the central tenet of that position has to do with Christ's empathy. First and foremost, of course, is the fact that Tupac's Jesus is black. The rap explains that Black Jesuz is "like a saint that we pray to" for the strength to endure life in the ghetto. Black Jesuz is "somebody that hurt like we hurt . . . drink like we drink, understand where we comin' from." "Black Jesuz" conveys the pragmatism of Tupac's religious stance, which hails not from theory, scripture, doctrine, or edict, but instead from the sheer need to survive in a hostile world. In fact, the rap treats holy writings with irreverence and suspicion ("wonder how shit like the Bible and the Koran was written / what is religion?"), since Tupac views them to be the man-made products of a corrupt system. His connection to Black Jesuz is completely unencumbered by all of the institutional trappings that society teaches us to attach to religion. Perhaps this simple, transparent cry for God's empathy is the purest religious expression of all. The link that Tupac perceives between his own suffering and the suffering of Christ may explain how the artist's religious conviction could seem to transcend all of his other personal challenges.

I emerged from my avowedly brief look into the world of Tupac with a newfound respect for what is called gangsta rap, as well as with a newfound conviction about the importance of this book. Many scholars have devoted considerable time and energy to discussing all that we, as African Americans, have lost, retained, and created as a result of our having been stripped from Africa. This study has shown that to a remarkable degree, we have retained the fused approach to music and religion characteristic of our ancestral, West-African worldview. Despite our attempts to polarize the sacred from the secular, we always end up praying to, thinking about, and preaching about God in our secular musical forms, a tendency I have cited in black secular music ranging from Bert Williams's minstrelsy to Tupac's raps. Perhaps we are no more able to conceive of music apart from religion—or vice versa—than were the Africans from whom we descend.

From this brief evidence, two things about Tupac's theosophy are clear: He trusted God's empathy, and he anticipated the afterlife. In a very powerful way, these two themes connect Tupac to the generations of black secular artists who preceded him. In particular, we can cite these themes in the music of the early blues artists who, like Tupac, birthed their music out of their troubled lives.

I believe that the extent of Tupac's story remains to be told. As of this writing, there are more articles and websites devoted to Tupac than one can count, and it seems that new ones are generated on a daily basis. It also seems that something of a cult has developed around the belief that Tupac really isn't dead after all, and websites devoted to this argument are too plentiful to cite here.[4] Suffice it to say, however, that I have recently encountered nearly a dozen websites that go into great detail to show evidence that Tupac faked his own death. Even before finding these, I entertained my own mild suspicions about the sudden proliferation of thought-provoking, posthumous releases that appeared before the rapper was lukewarm in his grave. The commercial music industry is sufficiently profit-driven these days that the notion of an incognito Tupac somewhere planning his thirty-first birthday bash is not entirely possible to rule out.

Even if Tupac really is dead as we suppose him to be, his legacy is very much alive. In an age when the commercialism of popular music makes it difficult to distinguish the manufactured from the genuine, Tupac Shakur takes on special significance. I believe that my students revered him because his blatant honesty was a welcome contrast to a culture filled with fakes, phonies, euphemisms, and tenuous, "virtual" realities. Tupac's legacy unites the most harrowing dimension of the African-American urban experience with the creative impulse of the black-American musical tradition. His legacy also underscores that paradoxical connection between the stain of poverty and the glitter of commercial success. Most important, perhaps, Tupac's legacy shows how the gangster, the thug, the outlaw, can fill our ears with bad words and ugly, brutal, truths, all the while pointing us to pictures of a caring God. This is the real meaning of fused dimensions, and to ascertain and to appreciate this fusion is to locate the holy within the profane.

NOTES

INTRODUCTION

1. See Portia Maultsby, "Africanisms in African American Music," 185–210. Maultsby shows the interconnected metamorphosis of three primary musical traditions: sacred, secular—non-jazz, and secular—jazz.

2. Laurenti Magesa, *African Religion*, 25.

3. Noel King, *Religion in Africa*, 10–11.

4. Magesa, *African Religion*, 35–36.

5. Patricia Carpenter, "Musical Object," 60; see also Edward Cone, *Musical Form and Musical Performance*, 13–16, for more on the Western approach to music.

6. Quoted in Eileen Southern, ed., *Readings in Black American Music*, 1–2.

7. John Webb, "Primal Roots of Jazz," 132.

8. Samuel Floyd, *Power of Black Music*, 32.

9. See Lawrence W. Levine, "Slave Songs and Slave Consciousness," 72.

10. Jeannette Robinson Murphy, "Survival of African Music," 662.

11. See Southern, ed, *Readings in Black American Music*, 61–63.

12. See Albert J. Raboteau, "Black Experience in American Evangelicalism," 91.

13. Charles C. Cole Jr., *Social Ideals of the Northern Evangelists*, 113–16.

14. C. Eric Lincoln and Lawrence H. Mamiya, *Black Church*, 78.

15. The phenomenon of *glossolalia* is described in Acts 2:1–4, Authorized (King James) Version.

16. See "Black Religious Tradition," in Harry A. Ploski and James Williams, eds., *Negro Almanac*, 1297–1332.

17. Raboteau, "Black Experience in American Evangelicalism," 98.

18. Eileen Southern, *Music of Black Americans*, 334.

19. "Enigmatic Folk Songs of the Southern Underworld." No author is cited, but the person quoted here is a Mr. Walter Kingsley.

20. See Alan Young, *Black Gospel Singers*, 9.

21. Daniel Wolff, *Sam Cooke*, 20–21.

22. Michael Harris, *Music of Thomas Andrew Dorsey*, 185.

23. Ibid.

24. Ibid., 97.

1. PENTECOSTALISM AND BLACK SECULAR MUSIC

1. Davin Seay and Mary Neely, *Spiritual Roots of Rock 'n' Roll*, 73.

2. See Dan Wakefield, "Speaking in Tongues," 98.

3. In this discussion, the terms *Holiness, Pentecostal, Sanctified,* and *Holiness/Pentecostal* are used interchangeably.

4. Quoted in Maultsby, "Africanisms in African American Music," 198.

5. See Southern, ed., *Readings in Black American Music,* 63–64.

6. Ibid., 105.

7. Quoted in Southern, *Music of Black Americans*, 182.

8. Ibid., 179.

9. Vinson Synan, *Holiness Pentecostal Tradition,* 12.

10. Southern, ed, *Readings in Black American Music,* 63–64.

11. Synan, *Holiness Pentecostal Tradition,* 13.

12. John Thomas Nichol, *Pentecostalism,* 18.

13. C.M. Robeck, "Azusa Street Revival."

14. Synan, *Holiness Pentecostal Tradition,* 100.

15. H.V. Synan, "William Joseph Seymour."

16. See Samuel Floyd, *Power of Black Music,* 20.

17. See Ithiel C. Clemmons, *Bishop C.H. Mason,* 31–32.

18. Clemons, *Bishop C.H. Mason,* 31.

19. See Alton Hornbsy, *Chronology of African American History.*

20. See Lincoln and Mamiya, *Black Church in the African American Experience,* 116.

21. See Southern, *Music of Black Americans,* 313–64.

22. Ibid., 332–34.

23. Dr. Frank Damrosch quoted in "Where is Jazz Leading America," 518.

24. See Nelson George, *Death of Rhythm and Blues,* x.

25. Seay and Neely, *Spiritual Roots of Rock and Roll,* 140.

26. Tina Turner with Kurt Loder, *I, Tina,* 21.

27 Portia Maultsby, "Impact of Gospel Music," 30.

28. The religious upbringing of the Debarge family is referenced in Michael Goldberg, "Debarge's Family Affair," 41. I am personally acquainted with Deniece Williams's religious roots. My mother attended Faith Temple Church of God in Christ where Williams was reared.

29. Harvey Cox, *Rise of Pentecostal Spirituality,* 142.

30. Jerma Jackson, "Politics of African-American Sacred and Secular Music," 153.

31. Clemmons, *Bishop C.H. Mason,* 21.

32. Ibid., 41–42.

33. Southern, *Music of Black Americans,* 378.

34. Clemmons, *Bishop C.H. Mason,* 84–100.

35. George, *Death of Rhythm and Blues,* 20.

36. Jannette L. Dates and William Barlow, eds, *African Americans in the Mass Media,* 81.

2. BLUES LYRICS

This chapter was previously accepted for publication in *Journal of Religious Thought,* 55, no. 2, and 56, no. 1 (1999), and is forthcoming as of this writing.

1. Some transcriptions are reprinted from Michael Taft, *Blues Lyric Poetry: An Anthology.* I also did some transcriptions from recordings made available by the Center for Popular Music at Middle Tennessee State University (Murfreesboro) and the Center for Black Music Research at Columbia University (Chicago).

2. Text as shown in Lydia Austin Parrish, *Slave Songs of the Georgia Sea Islands,* 134.

3. ELDER EATMORE AND DEACON JONES

This chapter was previously accepted for publication by *Popular Music and Society* and is forthcoming as of this writing.

1. See Chip Deffaa, *Six Lives in Rhythm and Blues,* 193.

2. See Robert Palmer, *Legendary Leiber and Stoller,* 13–19. Having written numerous hits for black performers, including Big Mama Thornton, Ruth Brown, the Coasters, the Drifters, the Isley Brothers and others, Leiber and Stoller forged their fame in the crucible of the black aesthetic. Jerry Leiber, born in 1933 in Baltimore, grew up on the edge of the city's black ghetto, where his mother owned the only store that, according to Leiber, was willing "to extend credit to black people." As he interacted with black families in the area, he developed a fascination with their culture. Mike Stoller, also born in 1933, grew up in a middle-class neighborhood in New York and once studied with black jazz great James P. Johnson. By the time Leiber and Stoller crossed paths in Los Angeles and began collaborating in 1950, they had already become "honorary blacks." Palmer writes: "More and more, Leiber and Stoller dropped out of conventional white society and began to identify themselves with the black subculture. They moved through a night world populated by jazzmen, black hipsters, and other stylish, creative, economically marginal types." Leiber states, "We found ourselves writing for black artists . . . because those were the voices and the rhythms we loved. By the fall of 1950 . . . we had black girlfriends and were into a black lifestyle" (p. 19). Their songs, such as "Broadway" and "Up on the Roof" hardly seem the product of two middle-class whites.

3. See Thomas Brothers's discussion of crossover as it relates to early blues in "Ideology and Aurality." See also Robert Kloosterman and Chris Quispel, "Analysis of Radio in Black Music." Kloosterman and Quispel state: "By the 1920s, much of the entertainment music played by white American musicians was clearly influenced by black music, but black and white music scenes were still segregated; black musicians played their songs for black audiences, whites played their music to all-white audiences" (p. 155).

4. H.K. Carroll, "Religious Progress of the Negro," 75.

5. Ibid., 81.

6. Ibid., 84.

7. Milton C. Sernett, *African American Religion and the Great Migration,* 161.

8. See William J. Mahar, *Early Blackface Minstrelsy.* Mahar's quote from p. 83. "Trip to a Nigga Meeting" quoted on pp. 83–84.

9. Michael Harris, *Music of Thomas Andrew Dorsey,* 122–23.

10. See Prince Dorough, *Popular Music Culture in America,* 75–77.

11. Jordan's father was a musician who toured with various minstrel shows. At the same time, the aunt with whom he lived was a pianist for the Mount Olive Baptist Church. Jordan was reared in the Baptist church, and it was there that he entertained some of his first audiences. Berle Adams quoted in John Chilton, *Louis Jordan and His Music,* 84.

12. Daryl Cumber Dance, Folklore from *Contemporary Black Americans,* 62.

13. Ibid., 64.

14. Horace Boyer, *Golden Age of Gospel,* 157.

15. This information was given to me by Ink Spots scholar and archivist Bill Proctor.

16. Marv Goldberg, *Ink Spots and Their Music,* 249.

17 . *Ebony* (Nov 1945): 21. Population statistics from "Annual Estimates of the Population by Sex and Race," in U.S. Department of the Commerce, *Historical Statistics of the United States.*

4. RETHINKING THE DEVIL'S MUSIC

1. Seay and Neely, *Spiritual Roots of Rock 'n' Roll,* 97.

2. Quoted in Gerri Hirshey, *Story of Soul Music,* 26.

3. Refer to the Introduction for a more thorough discussion of this topic.

4. Jon Michael Spencer, *Blues and Evil,* xxiii. *Peach orchard* and *jelly roll* were among the many euphemisms used in blues lyrics to refer to the female sex organ or to sex in general.

5. W.C. Handy, *Father of the Blues,* 10.

6. Quoted in Spencer, *Blues and Evil,* 28–29. Original source is Newbell Niles Puckett, *Folk Beliefs of the Southern Negro,* 554.

7. There are different versions of this story. Hirshey says that Johnson was poisoned by a jealous woman (100). Spencer says that Johnson's murderer was a husband or a girlfriend (10). While it's not exactly clear who committed the poisoning, his death was apparently related to some sort of love triangle.

8. Quoted in Arnold Shaw, *The Golden Years of Rhythm and Blues,* 303.

9. Throughout this discussion, the term *rhythm and blues* refers generically to black secular music from the late 1940s onward, although certain black artists and styles during the 1950s and 1960s might be more accurately categorized as *pop, rock 'n' roll,* or *soul.* Even though rhythm and blues usually refers

to black musical traditions, and rock 'n' roll to white traditions, most scholars would agree that in the mid to late 1950s and early 1960s these labels were virtually interchangeable.

10. See Brian Ward, *Rhythm and Blues, Black Consciousness, and Race Relations,* 59–60. The gospel and church roots of many northern doo-wop groups are cited in Todd R. Baptista, *Behind the Rhythm and the Blues.* Zola Taylor is quoted in Harry Weinger, "Platters' Glory Days," 12.

11. Lipsitz, "Creating Dangerously," xix.

12. Southern, *Music of Black Americans,* 464.

13. Horace Clarence Boyer, *The Golden Age of Gospel,* 110–11.

14. Kip Lornell, *African-American Sacred Vocal Harmony Quartets,* 33.

15. Spencer, *Blues and Evil,* 11.

16. James M. Salem, *Late, Great Johnny Ace,* 147.

17. Ibid., 117. A discussion of reverse covering is presented in Jim Haskins, *Biography of Dinah Washington,* 34–41. Dinah Washington eventually crossed over with "What A Difference a Day Makes."

18. Sam Cooke was an exception to this typical sequence. He went directly from gospel to pop music and was never really considered a rhythm-and-blues artist.

19. See Michael W. Harris, *Music of Thomas Andrew Dorsey,* 119. Harris quotes the following from the *Defender* editorial in question: "[Organizations] shall seek to instruct the migrants. As to the dress, habits and methods of living necessary to withstand the rigors of the northern climate. As to the efficiency, regularity, and application demanded of workers in the North. . . . Every Race man owes this to himself as well as to the newcomers, for what affects one affect[s] all. . . . It is your burden. Will you take it up?" In addition, *The Crisis,* edited by W.E.B. Dubois, was a regular proponent of Race progress, and numerous features published in the 1920s and 1930s called for blacks to advance themselves through economic and educational means.

20. These are all cited in Spencer, *Blues and Evil,* 116–17.

21. See Walter C. Daniel, *Richard B. Harrison and* The Green Pastures. Jernagin quoted in Barbara Dianne Savage, *Radio, War, and the Politics of Race,* 96.

22. Savage, *Radio, War, and the Politics of Race,* 40–41.

23. Ibid., 143.

24. Ibid., 42.

25. Ward, *Rhythm and Blues, Black Consciousness, and Race Relations,* 59–60.

26. May quoted in Wolff, *Sam Cooke,* 104–5.

27. King quoted in Ward, *Rhythm and Blues, Black Consciousness, and Race Relations,* 173.

28. Ray Allen, *African-American Sacred Quartets,* 78.

29. Ibid.

30. Ibid., 6.

31. Lornell, *African-American Sacred Vocal Harmony Quartets,* 32.
32. Ibid., 30–31.
33. Freed's earnings cited in Wolff, *Sam Cooke,* 93–94. Cole's earnings cited in Ward, *Rhythm and Blues, Black Consciousness, and Race Relations,* 133–34.
34. See Salem, *Late, Great Johnny Ace,* 25. Ace's income cited on page 77.
35. John Hammond, *John Hammond on Record,* 91. Although Hammond was an invited member of the NAACP for thirty years, the organization refused to sponsor his Spirituals to Swing concert, a watershed event presented first in 1938 and then in 1939 which exposed, among others, Sister Rosetta Tharpe to the mainstream public. Hammond was also instrumental in advancing the careers of Bessie Smith and Aretha Franklin.
36. Wolff, *Sam Cooke,* 130.
37. Ibid., 65.
38. Quoted in Shaw, *Golden Years of Rhythm and Blues,* 332–33.
39. Wolff, *Sam Cooke,* 104.
40. Jon Fitzgerald, "Motown Crossover Hits 1963–66."
41. See Hirshey, *Story of Soul Music,* 115.

5. EVOLUTION OF THE BLUES PREACHER

1. This and other biographical information on blues artists is available in a variety of sources including Sheldon Harris, ed., *Biographical Dictionary of Blues Singers* and Southern, *Biographical Dictionary of Afro-American and African Musicians.*
2. See Georges Balandier and Jacque Maquet, *Dictionary of Black African Civilization,* 161.
3. Stacey K. Close, "Religious Leadership in the Antebellum Slave Community," 64.
4. Ibid., 65.
5. Federal Writer's Project, *Slave Narratives,* 109.
6. Ibid., 169.
7. Southern, *Music of Black Americans,* 76–77.
8. Hamilton quoted in H. Beecher Hicks Jr., *Images of the Black Preacher,* 18.
9. See James H. Harris, *Black Ministers and Laity in the Urban Church,* 9–44.
10. Hicks, *Images of the Black Preacher,* 133–34.
11. Liner notes to *Preachin' the Gospel: Holy Blues,* Columbia/Legacy CK46779, 1991.
12. See Ward, *Rhythm and Blues, Black Consciousness, and Race Relations,* 179.
13. Liner notes, *Curtis Mayfield Gospel,* Rhino Entertainment Co. R275568, 1999.

14. Mayfield quoted in Ward, *Rhythm and Blues, Black Consciousness, and Race Relations,* 414.

15. Dolan Hubbard, *African American Literary Imagination,* 4–5.

16. See Peter Guralnick, *Sweet Soul Music,* 78. Guralnick says that the actual birth year is either 1936 or 1940. According to Ward, Burke was born in 1935 *(Rhythm and Blues, Black Consciousness, and Race Relations,* 199).

17. Guralnick, *Sweet Soul Music,* 78.

18. Burke quoted in Ward, *Rhythm and Blues, Black Consciousness, and Race Relations,* 199.

19. Guralnick, *Sweet Soul Music,* 81.

20. Burke's delivery here is highly reminiscent of the trademark spoken interludes in the music of the Mills Brothers.

21. Covay quoted in Guralnick, *Sweet Soul Music,* 85.

22. Ibid., 95.

23. See Ward, *Rhythm and Blues, Black Consciousness, and Race Relations,* 201.

24. Quoted in Bil Carpenter, "Staple Singers," 28.

25. As far as secular sermonizing goes, it is my opinion that Gaye's *What's Going On* has yet to be outdone.

26. David Ritz, *Life of Marvin Gaye,* 147.

27. Ibid., 147.

28. Jeffrey Peisch, *Stevie Wonder,* 8.

29. Quoted in John Swenson, *Stevie Wonder,* 22.

30. Hicks calls the title of the song "The Reverend Dr. Lee," but "Reverend Lee" is actually the correct title. The song was included on Roberta Flack's album, *Chapter Two,* which hit the album charts in August, 1970.

31. Hicks, *Images of the Black Preacher,* 135.

32. Marilyn Marshall, "Love Conquers All," 156.

33. Teddy Pendergrass and Patricia Romanowski, *Truly Blessed,* 32.

34. Ibid., 30.

35. Ibid., 31–32.

36. Ibid., 164.

37. Stacey Close, "Religious Leadership in the Antebellum Slave Community," 66.

38. Rickey Vincent, *Funk: The Music,* 4.

39. Ibid., 37.

40. Ibid., 138.

41. The primary source for all information included here on Sun Ra is John F. Szwed, *Lives and Times of Sun Ra.*

42. Ibid., 46.

43. Ibid., 92.

44. Ibid., 173–75.

45. Ibid, 155.

46. Ibid, 260.

47. Ibid, 262.

48. Ibid., 242.

49. John Rockwell, "Rock: A Funkadelic Yes and No," 41.

50. Robert Palmer, "Earth Wind and Fire at Garden," 78.

51. Quoted in Robert Windeler, "Higher Force," 57. Windeler describes Maurice Whites' upbringing in the Baptist Holiness Church.

52. Quoted in John Storm Roberts, "Earth, Wind, and Fire," 106.

53. Vivien Goldman, "Earth, Wind and Fire's Band of Hope," 37.

POSTLUDE: GOD AND GANGSTA RAP

1. This film, the story of a young, black fugitive running for his life, was called "an outrage" by *New York Times* reviewer Clayton Riley in 1971. See *New York Times Film Reviews,* 1971–1972, 62. The film's raw portrayal of what the same reviewer called "the ruined landscape of black life" was a shock to audiences viewing this treatment of sex, violence, and drugs.

2. Armond White cites Darryl James's comparison of Tupac Shakur to Marvin Gaye in *Rebel for the Hell of it: The Life of Tupac Shakur,* 184.

3. White, *Life of Tupac Shakur,* 126.

4. I hesitate to include websites in these notes, as they tend to be ephemeral, and, frequently, are of dubious origin.

BIBLIOGRAPHY

Allen, Ray. *Singing in the Spirit: African-American Sacred Quartets in New York City.* Philadelphia: Univ. of Pennsylvania Press, 1991.

Balandier, Georges, and Jacque Maquet. *Dictionary of Black African Civilization.* Trans. Peninah Neimark. New York: Leon Amiel, 1974.

Baptista, Todd R. *Group Harmony: Behind the Rhythm and the Blues.* New Bedford: TRB Enterp., 1996.

Boyer, Horace. *How Sweet the Sound: The Golden Age of Gospel.* Washington, D.C.: Elliott Clark, 1995.

Brothers, Thomas. "Ideology and Aurality in the Vernacular Traditions of African American Music, (ca. 1890–1950)." *Black Music Research Journal* 17, no. 2 (1997): 169–209.

Carpenter, Bil. "Staple Singers: God's Greatest Hitmakers." *Goldmine,* 30 Aug. 1996, 19.

Carpenter, Patricia. "The Musical Object." *Current Musicology* 5 (1967–1968): 56–87.

Carroll, H.K. "Religious Progress of the Negro." *Forum* 14 (Sept. 1892): 75–84.

Chilton, John. *Let the Good Times Roll: The Story of Louis Jordan and His Music.* Ann Arbor: Univ. of Michigan Press, 1994.

Clemmons, Ithiel C. *Bishop C.H. Mason and the Roots of the Church of God in Christ.* Bakersfield: Pneuma Life Pub., 1996.

Close, Stacey K. "Sending up Some Timber: Elderly Slaves and Religious Leadership in the Antebellum Slave Community." In *Black Religious Leadership from the Slave Community to the Million Man March,* ed. Felton O. Best, 61–72. Lewiston, N.Y: E. Mellen, 1998.

Cole, Charles C., Jr. *The Social Ideals of the Northern Evangelists, 1826–1860.* New York: Columbia Univ. Press, 1954.

Cone, Edward. *Musical Form and Musical Performance.* New York: Norton, 1968.

Cox, Harvey. *Fire from Heaven: The Rise of Pentecostal Spirituality and the Reshaping of Religion in the Twenty-First Century.* New York: Addison-Wesley, 1995.

Dance, Daryl Cumber. *Shuckin' and Jivin': Folklore from Contemporary Black Americans.* Bloomington: Indiana Univ. Press, 1978.

Daniel, Walter C. *De Lawd: Richard B. Harrison and* The Green Pastures. New York: Greenwood Pr., 1986.

Dates, Jannette L., and William Barlow, eds. *Split Image: African Americans in the Mass Media.* Washington, D.C.: Howard Univ. Press, 1990.

Deffaa, Chip. *Blue Rhythms: Six Lives in Rhythm and Blues.* Urbana: Univ. of Illinois Press, 1996.

Dorough, Prince. *Popular Music Culture in America.* New York: Ardsley, 1992.

"Enigmatic Folk Songs of the Southern Underworld: The Blues." *Current Opinion,* Sept. 1919, 165–66.

Federal Writer's Project. *Slave Narratives: A Folk History of Slavery in the United States, from Interviews with Former Slaves.* South Carolina Narratives, vol. 2, St. Clair Shores, Mich: Scholarly, 1976.

Fitzgerald, Jon. "Motown Crossover Hits 1963–66." *Popular Music* 14, no. 1 (1995): 1–11.

Floyd, Samuel. *The Power of Black Music: Interpreting Its History from Africa to the United States.* New York: Oxford Univ. Press, 1995.

Genovese, Eugene D. *Roll, Jordan, Roll: The World the Slaves Made.* New York: Vintage Bks., 1974.

George, Nelson. *The Death of Rhythm and Blues.* New York: E.P. Dutton, 1989.

Goldberg, Marv. *More Than Words Can Say: The Ink Spots and Their Music.* Lanham, Md: Scarecrow, 1998.

Goldberg, Michael. "Debarge's Family Affair: Motown Spawns Another Jackson 5." *Rolling Stone,* 26 Apr. 1984, 41.

Goldman, Vivien. "Earth, Wind and Fire's Band of Hope." *Melody Maker,* 10 Mar. 1979, 37.

Guralnick, Peter. *Sweet Soul Music: Rhythm and Blues and the Southern Dream of Freedom.* Boston: Little, Brown, 1999.

Hammond, John. *John Hammond on Record: An Autobiography.* New York: Penguin, 1981.

Handy, W.C. *Father of the Blues.* New York: Macmillan, 1951.

Harris, James H. *Black Ministers and Laity in the Urban Church: An Analysis of Political and Social Expectations.* Lanham, Md.: Univ. Press of America, 1987.

Harris, Michael W. *The Rise of Gospel Blues: The Music of Thomas Andrew Dorsey in the Urban Church.* New York: Oxford, 1992.

Harris, Sheldon, ed. *Blues Who's Who: A Biographical Dictionary of Blues Singers.* New Rochelle, N.Y: Arlington Hse., 1979.

Haskins, Jim. *Queen of the Blues: A Biography of Dinah Washington.* New York: W. Morrow, 1987.

Hicks, H. Beecher, Jr. *Images of the Black Preacher: The Man Nobody Knows.* Valley Forge, Pa.: Judson, 1977.

Hirshey, Gerri. *Nowhere to Run: The Story of Soul Music.* New York: Da Capo, 1994.

Hornsby, Alton. *Chronology of African American History.* Detroit: Gale Res., 1991.

Hubbard, Dolan. *The Sermon and the African American Literary Imagination.* Columbia: Univ. of Missouri Press, 1994.

Jackson, Jerma. "Testifying at the Cross: Thomas Andrew Dorsey, Sister Rosetta Tharpe, and the Politics of African-American Sacred and Secular Music." Ph.D. diss., Rutgers, State Univ. of New Jersey, 1995.

King, Noel. *African Cosmos: An Introduction to Religion in Africa.* Belmont: Wadsworth Pub., 1986.

Kloosterman, Robert, and Chris Quispel. "Not Just the Same Old Show on My Radio: An Analysis of the Role of Radio in the Diffusion of Black Music Among Whites in the South of the United States of America, 1920–1960." *Popular Music* 9, no. 2 (1990): 151–64.

Levine, Lawrence W. "Slave Songs and Slave Consciousness." In *African-American Religion: Interpretive Essays in History and Culture,* ed. Timothy E. Fulop and Albert J. Raboteau, 57–88. New York: Routledge, 1997.

Lincoln, C. Eric, and Lawrence H. Mamiya. *The Black Church in the African-American Experience.* Durham: Duke Univ. Press, 1990.

Lipsitz, George. "Creating Dangerously: The Blues Life of Johnny Otis," pp. xvii–xxxv. Introduction to *Upside Your Head: Rhythm and Blues on Central Avenue,* by Johnny Otis. Hanover: Wesleyan Univ. Press, 1993.

Lornell, Kip. *Happy in the Service of the Lord: African-American Sacred Vocal Harmony Quartets in Memphis,* 2d ed. Knoxville: Univ. of Tennessee Press, 1995.

Magesa, Laurenti. *African Religion: The Moral Traditions of Abundant Life.* Maryknoll: Orbis Bks., 1997.

Mahar, William J. *Behind the Burnt Cork Mask: Early Blackface Minstrelsy and Antebellum American Popular Culture.* Urbana: Univ. of Illinois Press, 1999.

Marshall, Marilyn. "Love Conquers All." *Ebony,* Feb. 1989, 156.

Maultsby, Portia. "The Impact of Gospel Music on the Secular Music Industry." In *We'll Understand it Better By and By: Pioneering African American Gospel Composers,* ed. Bernice Johnson Reagon, 19–33. Washington, D.C.: Smithsonian, 1992.

———. "Africanisms in African American Music." In *Africanisms in African-American Culture,* ed. Joseph E. Holloway, 185–210. Bloomington: Indiana Univ. Press, 1990.

Murphy, Jeannette Robinson. "The Survival of African Music in America." *Popular Science Monthly* 55 (Sept. 1899): 660–72.

New York Times Film Reviews, 1971–1972. New York: New York Times, 1973.

Nichol, John Thomas. *Pentecostalism.* New York: Harper and Row, 1966.

Nketia, J. H. Kwabena. *The Music of Africa.* London: V. Gollancz, 1975.

Otis, Johnny. *Upside Your Head: Rhythm and Blues on Central Avenue.* Hanover: Wesleyan Univ. Press, 1993.

Palmer, Robert. *Baby That Was Rock 'n' Roll: The Legendary Leiber and Stoller.* New York: Harcourt Brace Jovanovich, 1978.

———. "Earth Wind and Fire at Garden with New Song-Oriented Show." *New York Times,* 27 Nov. 1977, p.78.

Parrish, Lydia Austin. *Slave Songs of the Georgia Sea Islands.* Hatboro, Pa.: Folklore Assoc., 1965.

Peisch, Jeffrey. *Stevie Wonder.* New York: Ballantine, 1985.

Pendergrass, Teddy, and Patricia Romanowski. *Truly Blessed.* New York: G.P. Putnam, 1998.

Ploski, Harry A., and James Williams, eds. In *The Negro Almanac: A Reference Work on the African American,* 5th ed. Detroit: Gale Res., 1989.

Puckett, Newbell Niles. *Folk Beliefs of the Southern Negro.* Chapel Hill: Univ. of North Carolina Press, 1926.

Raboteau, Albert J. "The Black Experience in American Evangelicalism: The Meaning of Slavery." In *African-American Religion: Interpretive Essays in History and Culture,* ed. Timothy E. Fulop and Albert J. Raboteau, 89–106. New York: Routledge, 1997.

Ritz, David. *Divided Soul: The Life of Marvin Gaye.* New York: McGraw-Hill, 1985.

Robeck, C.M. "Azusa Street Revival." In *Dictionary of Pentecostal and Charismatic Movements,* ed. Stanley M. Burgess and Gary B. McGee, 31–36, Grand Rapids: Zondervan, 1988.

Roberts, John Storm. "Earth, Wind, and Fire—Mystagogic Funk." *Hi Fidelity Magazine,* Jan. 1979, 103–6.

Rockwell, John. "Rock: A Funkadelic Yes and No." *New York Times,* 12 Sept. 1977, 41.

Salem, James M. *The Late, Great Johnny Ace and the Transition from R&B to Rock and Roll.* Urbana: Univ. of Illinois Press, 1999.

Savage, Barbara Dianne. *Broadcasting Freedom: Radio, War, and the Politics of Race, 1938–1948.* Chapel Hill: Univ. of North Carolina Press, 1999.

Seay, Davin, and Mary Neely. *Stairway to Heaven: The Spiritual Roots of Rock 'n' Roll—From the King and Little Richard to Prince and Amy Grant.* New York: Ballantine Epiphany, 1986.

Sernett, Milton C. *Bound for the Promised Land: African American Religion and the Great Migration.* Durham: Duke Univ. Press, 1997.

Shaw, Arnold. *Honkers and Shouters: The Golden Years of Rhythm and Blues.* New York: Macmillan, 1978.

Southern, Eileen. *Biographical Dictionary of Afro-American and African Musicians.* Westport, Connecticut: Greenwood Pr., 1982.

———. *The Music of Black Americans: A History,* 3d ed. New York: Norton, 1997.

————, ed. *Readings in Black American Music.* New York: Norton, 1971.

Spencer, Jon Michael. *Blues and Evil.* Knoxville: Univ. of Tennessee Press, 1993.

Swenson, John. *Stevie Wonder.* New York: Harper and Row, 1986.

Synan, H.V. "William Joseph Seymour." In *Dictionary of Pentecostal and Charismatic Movements,* ed. Stanley M. Burgess and Gary B. McGee, 778–81. Grand Rapids: Zondervan, 1988.

Synan, Vinson. *The Holiness Pentecostal Tradition: Charismatic Movements in the Twentieth Century.* Grand Rapids: Eerdmans, 1997.

Szwed, John F. *Space is the Place: The Lives and Times of Sun Ra.* New York: Pantheon, 1997.

Taft, Michael. *Blues Lyric Poetry: An Anthology.* New York: Garland Publ., 1983.

Turner, Tina, with Kurt Loder. *I, Tina.* New York: W. Morrow, 1986.

U.S. Department of the Commerce, Bureau of the Census. "Annual Estimates of the Population by Sex and Race." In *Historical Statistics of the United States: Colonial Times to 1970, Part I,* 9. Washington, D.C., 1975.

Vincent, Rickey. *Funk: The Music, the People, and the Rhythm of the One.* New York: St. Martin Griffin, 1996.

Wakefield, Dan. "Speaking in Tongues." *Nation,* 23 Jan. 1995, 98–101.

Ward, Brian. *Just My Soul Responding: Rhythm and Blues, Black Consciousness, and Race Relations.* Berkeley: Univ. of California Press, 1998.

Webb, John. "The Primal Roots of Jazz: Rediscovering the Music of Vodou." In *Jazz Research Papers,* ed. Larry Fischer, 128–35. Manhattan, Kans.: Natl. Assoc. of Jazz Educators, 1995.

Weinger, Harry. "The Platters' Glory Days." *Goldmine,* 21 Feb. 1992, 10–14.

"Where Is Jazz Leading America?" *Etude* 42 (Aug. 1924): 518.

White, Armond. *Rebel for the Hell of It: The Life of Tupac Shakur.* New York: Thunders Mouth, 1997.

Windeler, Robert. "'A Higher Force' is the Tenth Member of Maurice White's Ascetic Earth, Wind and Fire." *People,* 8 Nov. 1976, 56–57.

Wolff, Daniel. *You Send Me.* New York: W. Morrow, 1995.

Young, Alan. *Woke Me Up This Morning: Black Gospel Singers and the Gospel Life.* Jackson: Univ. of Mississippi Press, 1997.

SELECTED RECORDINGS

Alexander, Texas. "Sittin' on a Log." Okeh 8624, 1928.

Arnold, Kokomo. "The Twelves." Decca 7083, 1935.

Bailey, Mildred. "Is That Religion?" Brunswick 6558, 1933.

Bailey, Mildred. "Shoutin' in the Amen Corner." Brunswick 6655, 1933.

Baker, LaVern. "Saved." Atlantic 45–2099, 1961.

Brown, Hi Henry. "Preacher Blues." Vocalion 1728, 1932.

Chatman, Peter. "Lend Me Your Love." Bluebird B9028, 1941.

Cox, Ida. "Fogyism." Riverside Jazz Archives RLP 147, 1928.

Dickson, Pearl. "Little Rock Blues." Columbia 14286, 1927.

Ellington, Duke. "Sing, You Sinners." Hit of the Week 1045, 1930.

Ellington, Duke. "Is That Religion?" Mellotone M-12080, 1931.

Harris, Wynonie. "The Deacon Don't Like It." King 4635, 1953.

House, Son. "Preachin' the Blues." Parts 1 and 2. Paramount 13013, 1930.

Jackson, Jim. "I Heard the Voice of a Porkchop." Victor 21387, 1928.

Jordan, Louis. "Deacon Jones." Decca 8654, 1943.

Millinder, Lucky. "Fare Thee Well, Deacon Jones." Decca 24495, 1946.

McTell, Blind Willie. "Broke Down Engine." Vocalion 02577, 1933.

McTell, Blind Willie. "Southern Can is Mine." Columbia 14632, 1931.

The Orioles. "Deacon Jones." Jubilee 5005, 1949.

Phillips, Little Esther. "The Deacon Moves In." Federal 12016, 1951.

Stevens, Vol. "Stonewall Blues." (Recording by the Memphis Jug Band.) Bluebird B5675, 1930.

Stokes, Frank. "You Shall." Paramount 12518, 1927.

Tharpe, Rosetta. "Rock Me." Document DOCD 5335, 1943.

Tharpe, Rosetta. "Strange Things Happening Every Day." Decca 8669, 1944.

Torey, George. "Lonesome Man Blues." American Record Corporation 7–08–57, 1937.

Williams, Bert. "Oh Death, Where is Thy Sting!" Columbia A2652, 1918.

Williams, Bert. "Elder Eatmore's Sermon's on Generosity and Throwing Stones." Columbia A6141, 1919.

Williams, Joe. "Mr. Devil Blues." Vocalion 1457, 1929.

Wilson, Kid Wesley. "The Gin Done Done It." Columbia 14463, 1929.

INDEX

Ace, Johnny, 93, 96, 104, 108
Adams, Berle, 79
African Methodist Episcopal Church, 116
Alexander, Reverend John, 104
Alexander, J.W., 109
Alexander, Leslie, 96–97
Alexander, Texas, 60
"All About Love," 146
"All Coons Look Alike to Me," 24
Allen, Richard, 116
"All I Want Is That Pure Religion," 10
Alphatones, 122
"Amen," 122–23
America Eats Its Young, 143
Americans All, Immigrants All, 99–101
Anderson, Marian, 149
Apollo (records), 95, 124
Apollo Theater, 107, 109
Arkestra, 140–41. *See also* Cosmic Space Jazz Group; Solar-Hieroglyphics Arkestra; Intergalactic Research Arkestra; Astro-Solar Arkestra
Armstrong, Louis, 85
Arnold, Kokomo, 46, 51
ASCAP, 27, 35
Assemblies of God, 35
Astrology, 141
Astro Solar Arkestra, 140. *See also* Arkestra; Cosmic Space Jazz Group; Solar-Hieroglyphics Arkestra; Intergalactic Research Arkestra
Atlantic Records, 125

Azusa Street revival, 8, 16, 21, 23, 34–36

"Baby, Let Me Lay It on You," 113
Baadasssss, 151
"Bad Luck," 136
Bailey, Mildred, 78
Baker, Anita, xi
Baker, LaVern, 33, 63, 77, 87, 103
Ballard, Hank, 95
Baptist Holiness Church (Memphis, Tennessee), 143, 168 n 51
Baptists, African-American:
  compared to Pentecostals, 34;
  conflict with Pentecostals, 35; in
  "Preachin' the Blues," 55;
  church membership, 56; in
  Chicago, 69; and storefront
  churches, 70; and "Reverend,"
  74; in deacon caricature tunes,
  82; clergymen in the Civil Rights
  Movement, 87; and Clyde
  McPhatter, 93; and Reverend
  Rubin Lacy, 114; in "Denomina-
  tion Blues," 119; and imagery in
  sacred songs, 123; and "Reverend
  Lee," 133; and Herman Blount
  (Sun Ra), 138
Bar-kays, 30–32, 137
Basie, Count, 27
Bates, Deacon L.J., 10, 91, 113, 118.
  See also Brown, Elder J.C.;
  Jefferson, Blind Lemon
Bell, Al, 128
Belvin, Jesse, 96, 109
Berry, Chuck, 28

Bethel Pentecostal Church (Grand
    Rapids, Michigan), 33
biblical imagery in the blues, 42–50
Biggie Small, 154. *See also* Christo-
    pher Wallace
Billboard, 102, 111
Birmingham Jubilee Singers, 77
"Black Boy," 100
black church: focal point of African-
    American life, 50–51; gender
    imbalance in, 52; of the 1920s,
    53; in Chicago, 69; in "Is That
    Religion?" 78; and civil rights
    meetings, 87; and training of
    rhythm-and-blues artists, 93–95;
    as portrayed in *The Negro Soldier,*
    100, 106; defection of artists
    from, 102; in secular material,
    111; and secular music of the mid
    1960s, 112; and Curtis Mayfield,
    122–23; and message songs, 127–
    28; and Sun Ra, 141; and Maurice
    White, 145–46
blackface entertainers, 70. *See also*
    minstrelsy
Black Herman, 138
"Black Jesuz," 158
Blackwell, Bumps, 109–10
blaxploitation films, 151
Bledsoe, Jules, 100
Blount, Herman, 138–39. *See also*
    Sun Ra
"Boogie Wonderland," 145
Bootsy's Rubber Band, 137, 141–42
Boston G-Clefs, 93
Boyd, David, 119
"Brenda's Got a Baby," 156–58
Brewer, Blind James, 35
"Broadway," 163 n 3.2
"Broke Down Engine," 41
Brown, Hi Henry, 51–52
Brown, James, 12, 14; and
    Pentecostalism, 15, 28, 33; and
    the Famous Flames, 93; and the
    gospel ethos, 104, 121
Brown, Elder J.C., 113. *See also*

Jefferson, Blind Lemon; Bates,
    Deacon L.J.
Brown, Ruth, 12, 92, 163 n 2.2
Brown v. Board of Education, 121
Bryant's Jubilee Quartet, 77
Bu Allah (Muslim slave), 137
Buddhism, 143
Burke, Solomon, 112, 124–27, 167
    nn 16, 20
Burnett, Chester, 92. *See also*
    Howlin' Wolf
Burnett, Reverend J.C., 10
bush meeting, 68. *See also* camp
    meeting

call-and-response: in Pentecostal
    singing, 23; in "Shout!" 31; in
    "Strange Things Happening
    Everyday," 84; and "Sh-boom,"
    102; in "People Get Ready," 123;
    and speech-song of black preach-
    ing, 125
camp meeting, 7, 68: Cane Ridge, 19;
    interracial contact in, 36, 64; and
    minstrelsy, 70; and slave preachers,
    116. *See also* bush meeting
Cannon, Gus, 113
Carnegie Hall, 136
Catholic church, 93
"Change Is Gonna Come, A," 112
chanting, 4, 142–43
Chapter Two, 167 n 30
Charles, Ray, 104
Chatman, Peter, 44–45
Chicago Defender, 86, 98, 165 n 19
Chords, 102
Church of Christ (Holiness), 8, 21
Church of God in Christ, 8: founding
    of, 21–22; and secular artists, 33–
    35; referenced in blues lyrics, 52;
    and Rosetta Tharpe, 82–84; and
    blues artists, 113
Church of the Living God, 8
Civil Rights Movement, 36, 38: and
    deacon caricature tunes, 87; and
    the black church, 105; and change

in black religious consciousness, 118, 121

Clara Ward Singers, 95, 107

Clinton, George, 137, 142–43

"Close the Door," 134

Coasters, 163 n 3.2

"Cocaine Blues," 113

Cole, Bob, 25

Cole, Nat King, 108

Columbia Records, 97, 114

Commodores, 137

conjuring, 136, 137

Connelly, Marc 99

Cooke, Reverend Charles, 104

Cooke, Sam, 12, 28: and crossing over, 89–90, 103–4, 109–10, 120; death of, 96; "That's Heaven to Me," 105–6; "A Change Is Gonna Come," 112

Cosby Show, 157

Cosmic Space Jazz Group, 140. *See also* Arkestra; Solar-Hieroglyphics Arkestra; Intergalactic Research Arkestra; Astro-Solar Arkestra

Cotton Club, 34

covering, 97

Cox, Ida, 59

crossing over, 13, 90, 97: jazz as crossover genre, 27; and Louis Jordan, 79; in the 1950s, 111, 120, 151; and Motown, 112; and the Staple Singers, 127

The Crisis, 165 n 19

Crutcher, Bettye, 127–28

"Cry to Me," 125–26

Current Opinion, 9

Daughtry, Reverend Herbert, 152–53

Davis, Reverend Blind Gary, 55, 113

"Deacon Brown Is Dead!" 81

"Deacon Don't Like It, The," 80

"Deacon Jones," 79–80

"Deacon Moves In, The," 80, 84, 134

"Dear Mama," 153

Death Row Records, 149

Debarge, 12, 33, 162 n 28

Decca Records, 82, 84

deejay, 87, 97

"Denomination blues," 119–20

Dickson, Pearl, 57

Dixie Hummingbirds, 84

dolceola, 119

Dominoes, 80, 93, 104, 120

"Don Juan," 63

doo-wop groups, 93, 102, 120, 165 n 10

Dorsey, Thomas, 10–11, 27, 56–57, 82, 95. *See also* Georgia Tom

"Downfall of Nebuchadnezzar, The," 10

"Down in the Valley," 126

"Do You Call That Religion?" 77

Drifters, 163 n 3.2

DuBois, W.E.B., 100, 165 n 19

Earth, Wind, and Fire, 137–38, 141–46

Egyptology, 118, 139–41, 143–44

Elder Eatmore Sermons, 74, 78

El-Dorados, 139

Ellington, Duke, 27, 75, 77

Emotions, 145

Europe, James Reese, 25

Evangelicalism: compared to Holiness and Pentecostalism, 7–8; and the black church, 51; preachers, 55; and black and white revivalist traditions, 75; whites, 76; and sacred/secular distinction, 90. *See also* Holiness; Pentecostalism; Sanctified church

Evers, Medgar, 121

Faith Temple Church of God in Christ (East Chicago, Ind.), x, 33, 162 n 28

"Fare Thee Well, Deacon Jones," 79–80

Federal Writer's Project, 116

Five Royales, 92. *See also* Royal Sons

Flack, Roberta, 12, 133, 167 n 30

Flowers, Evangelist Mary, 114. *See also* Miles, Josephine
"Fogyism," 59
Fossett, Calvin, 93
Francis, David "Panama," 33
Franklin, Aretha, 33, 112, 121, 166 n 35
Franklin, Reverend C.L., 104
Fraternal Council of Negro Churches, 99
Freed, Alan, 108
freewill offerings, x, 94, 95, 106
Fuller, Blind Boy, 10. *See also* Brother George and His Sanctified Singers
funk, 137–38, 143

gangsta rap, 149, 150, 158
Gaye, Marvin, 12: and the Pentecostal tradition, 28; tragic death of, 96; and message songs, 127–28; *What's Going On,* 129–30, 151; compared to Tupac, 152, 156
George, Nelson, 151
Georgia Tom, 10, 57. *See also* Thomas Dorsey
"Gin Done Done It, The," 52–54
glossolalia: origin, 8, 16, 161 n 15; in worship, 19, 21; in "Holy Ghost," 32. *See also* speaking in tongues
"God Bless the Dead," 153–55
Gordy, Berry, 129
gospel blues, 10–11, 56
Gospel Minnie (Lizzie Douglas), 91. *See also* Memphis Minnie
Gospel Starlighters, 92. *See also* James Brown
Gospel Tornadoes, 93. *See also* Silhouettes
Graham Central Station, 137
Green Pastures, The, 99–100
griot, 114–16
guitar (as "the Devil's instrument"), 119

"Hail Mary," 155

"Hallelujah, I Love Her So," 104
Hallelujah Joe, 114. *See also* McCoy, Joe
Hall Negro Quartet, 77
Hammond, John, 109, 166 n 35
Handy, W.C., 35, 65, 91
Harlemaires, 93
Harlem Church of God in Christ, 34
Harlem Hot Chocolates, 75
Harlem Renaissance, 38, 100
Harold Melvin and the Blue Notes, 134
Harris, Wynonie, 80
Hathaway, Donny, 96
"Have Mercy, Baby," 104
"Have Mercy, Lord," 104
Hawkins, Screaming Jay, 33
"Hellhound on My Trail," 92
"Hide Me in Thy Bosom," 82. *See also* "Rock Me"
Higgins, Godfrey, 139
"Higher Ground," 131
Hogan, Ernest, 24–25
Holiday, Billie, 152
Holiness: compared to Evangelicalism and Pentecostalism, 7, 8, 16; worship practices, 22–23, 33–34; artists reared in, 33; in "Preacher Blues," 51–52; and minstrelsy, 69–70, 74; and Teddy Pendergrass, 135. *See also* Evangelicalism; Pentecostalism; Sanctified church
holy blues, 119. *See also* preaching blues
holy dance, x, 32. *See also* shout
"Holy Ghost," 29, 31–32
Holy Spirit possession, 15, 37. *See also* spirit possession
House of God for All People, 124
House of God, the Holy Church of the Living God, the Pillar and Ground of the Truth, the House of Prayer for All People, 128–29
House of the Lord Church (Brooklyn, New York), 152

House, Son, 55–58, 91
Houston, Cissy, 90
Houston, Whitney, 12
Howlin' Wolf, 92. *See also* Chester
    Burnett
"How Long Will They Mourn Me?"
    154
Hudson, James "Pookie," 93
"Humpty Dumpty Heart," 103
Hurt, Mississippi John, 55

"If You Need Me," 126
"If You See My Savior," 56
"I Got a Woman," 104
"I Heard the Voice of a Porkchop,"
    65
"I Heard the Voice of Jesus Say," 65
Ihnfinity, Inc., 139, 141
"I'm Hanging Up My Heart for You,"
    126
Impressions, 122
Ink Spots, 85–86
"Inner City Blues," 129, 152
Innervisions, 131, 133
Intergalactic Research Arkestra, 140.
    See also Arkestra; Cosmic Space
    Jazz Group; Solar-Hieroglyphics
    Arkestra; Astro-Solar Arkestra
Intergroup Strategy, 99
Interscope Records, 153
"In the Stone," 145
"I Put a Spell on You," 33
Islam, 118, 140–42. *See also* Muslim
    faith
Isley Brothers, 29, 30, 32, 163 n 3.2
"Is That Religion?" 77–78
"I Want to Be Like Jesus in My
    Heart," 10
"I Wish I Knew (How It Would Feel
    to Be Free)," 127

Jackson, Jim, 65
Jackson, John G., 139
Jackson, Mahalia, 27, 107
James, George G.M., 139
Jefferson, Blind Lemon, 10, 55, 91,

113, 118. *See also* Bates, Deacon
    L.J.; Brown, Elder J.C.
Jernagin, Reverend W.H., 99
"Jesus Children of America," 131
Johnson, James, P., 163 n 3.2
Johnson, James Weldon, 25
Johnson, J. Rosamond, 25
Johnson, Robert, 91–92, 96, 156
jokelore, 81, 86, 151
Jones, Charles Price, 21, 35
Jones, Ruth Lee, 92. *See also*
    Washington, Dinah
Joplin, Scott, 24, 35, 59, 149
Jordan, Louis: church roots, 12, 92,
    164 n 11; jump blues, 28; "Dea-
    con Jones," 78–79; and "deacon"
    tunes, 120
"Just Out of Reach (Of My Two
    Open Arms)," 125–26

Keen Records, 109
"Keep on Pushing," 122
"Keep Ya Head Up," 152, 156
Kentucky Jubilee Four, 77
King, B.B., 12, 28
King, Ben E., 104
King, Martin Luther, Jr., 36, 105, 130
Knight, Gladys, 12, 33
kora, 114
Kool and the Gang, 137
Ku Klux Klan, 130

LaBelle, Patti, 33
Lacy, Reverend Rubin, 114
Leiber, Jerry, 63, 163 n 3.2
"Lend Me Your Love," 44–45
"Let's Hear It for the Boy," xi
Lewis, Furry, 113
Lewis, Jerry Lee, 28
Lewis, Ramsey, 143
Little Richard, 28, 89, 104. *See also*
    Penniman, Richard
"Little Rock Blues," 57
"Living for the City," 131
Locke, Alain, 100
"Lonesome Man Blues," 44

Lymon, Frankie, 93
Lymon, Frankie, Sr., 93
Lymon, Lewis and the Teen Chords, 93

Maggot Brain, 143
Martha and the Vandellas, 104
Martin, Roberta, 95, 107
Martin, Sallie, 95
Mason, Charles Harrison, 21–22, 35
Mason Temple Church of God in
    Christ (Memphis, Tennessee), 36
Massey, Gerald, 139
Mathis, Johnny, x
May, Brother Joe, 105, 107
Mayfield, Curtis, 111–12, 121–24,
    126–27
McCoy, Joe, 114. *See also* Hallelujah
    Joe
McPhatter, Clyde, 93, 96
McTell, Blind Willie, 41, 49, 51
"Me and the Devil Blues," 92, 156
"Memphis Blues," 35
Memphis Minnie (Lizzie Douglas),
    91. *See also* Gospel Minnie
Mercury Records, 97
"Mercy Mercy Me," 129
message song, 127–28, 130, 152
Methodists, African American, 17,
    19, 34, 92, 119
*Methodist Error or Friendly Chris-
    tian Advice to Those Methodists
    Who Indulge in Extravagant
    Religious Emotions and Bodily
    Exercises,* 16–17
migration of African Americans: in
    1910s, 23, 74; during World War
    II, 35; and storefront churches,
    68; and religious caricature, 77–
    78; and black church life, 86, 94,
    120; and secularization, 98, 104–5
Miles, Josephine, 114. *See also*
    Flowers, Evangelist Mary
Millinder, Lucky, 79–80, 82, 87
Mills, Irving, 75, 77
Mills Brothers, 85, 167 n 20

minstrelsy, 24, 70–74, 78, 86, 164 n
    11
Moonglows, 139
Moore, Arnold "Gatemouth," 34, 114
Moss, Carlton, 100
Mother Ship, 140. *See also*
    Mothership
Mothership, 142. *See also* Mother
    Ship
Motown, 112, 129
"Move on Up a Little Higher," 107
"Mr. Devil Blues," 41, 47–48
Muslim faith, 137. *See also* Islam
"My Black Mama," 58

NAACP, 166 n 35
National Baptist Convention, 10, 56
National Camp Meeting Association
    for the Promotion of Holiness, 7
National Convention of the Churches
    of God, Holiness, 8
Negro Soldier, The, 100, 106
Negro spiritual: slaves' use of, 5;
    compared to blues, 9, 39, 42–43,
    57; and religious stigma, 98;
    imagery in, 112, 122; and funk,
    141–42; and "Hail Mary," 155
"Ninety-Nine and a Half," 104
"Norah, Hist the Windah," 42
Northern Jubilee Gospel Choir, 122
"Nowhere to Run," 104

"Oh Death, Where Is Thy Sting?" 74
Ohio Players, 137
"Only You," 103
Open Our Eyes, 145
oral tradition, 42, 65, 115
Orioles, 80
orisha, 4, 22
Otis, Johnny, 37, 93
Outlawz, 158

Paramount, 114
Parham, Charles F., 16, 19
Parliament-Funkadelic, 137–38,
    141–42

Patton, Charlie, 10, 27, 91. *See also*
   Elder J.J. Handley
Peeples, Melvin Van, 151
Pendergrass, Teddy, 134–36
Penniman, Richard. *See* Little
   Richard
Pentecostalism: compared to
   Evangelicalism and Holiness, 7–
   8; and glossolalia, 15–16;
   American fathers of, 19–22;
   worship style, 22–23; influence on
   secular artists, 28–34; minstrel
   parodies of, 70–74; and Rosetta
   Tharpe, 82–85; and Marvin Gaye,
   129. *See also* Evangelicalism;
   Holiness; Sanctified church
"People Get Ready," 112, 122–23
Phillips, Little Esther, 80, 94, 120
Phillips, Washington, 55, 119
Pickett, Wilson, 104
"Pilgrim of Sorrow," 112
Pinewood Tom, 114. *See also* Joshua
   White
Pirouette (records), 85
Pitts, Reverend Alfred, 113. See also
   Johnny Watson
Platters, 93, 103, 111
pop charts, 63, 102, 125, 129–30
"Preacher blues," 51
"Preachin' the Blues," Parts 1 and 2,
   55–57
preaching blues, 119. *See also* holy
   blues
"Precious Lord, Take My Hand," 10
Presbyterians, 119
Presley, Elvis, 28
"Price, The," 125
Price, Florence, 101
Process Church of the Final Judg-
   ment, 143
pseudonyms, use of, 10, 113, 118–19

race music, 27, 65
Radio, 25, 35, 87, 95, 107
Rainey, "Ma" (Gertrude), 10, 25
"Rapper's Delight," 150

Rapture, xi
Rawls, Lou, 109
Redding, Otis, 96
"Respect Yourself," 130, 151
"Reverend Lee," 133–34, 167 n 30
rhythm-and-blues charts, 63, 111,
   125, 130
ring shout, 18. *See also* shout
"Rock Me," 82, 84. *See also* "Hide
   Me in Thy Bosom"
Roman Catholicism, 4
Roosters, 122
Rose, Tricia, 151
Royal Sons, 92. *See also* Five
   Royales
Rupe, Art, 109

Sallie Martin Singers, 92
"Sally, Where'd You Get the Liquor
   From?" 113
Sanctified church, 28, 29, 92, 94,
   133. *See also* Evangelicalism;
   Holiness; Pentecostalism
"Saved," 63–64, 77, 87
Savoy (records), 95
Schiffman, Bob, 109
"See See Rider," 33
Seventh-Day Adventists, 139
Seymour, William J., 8, 16, 19, 21,
   35–36
Shakur, Afeni, 152, 157
Shakur, Tupac, 149, 150; early life,
   151–52; compared to Marvin
   Gaye, 152; "Keep Ya Head Up,"
   152; "Dear Mama," 153; "God
   Bless the Dead," 153–55; and
   Reverend Daughtry, 153; "How
   Long Will They Mourn Me?" 154;
   rivalry with Biggie Small (Chris-
   topher Wallace), 154; "Hail
   Mary" and "God Bless the Dead,"
   155; compared to Robert Johnson,
   156; "Unconditional Love," 156;
   "Brenda's Got a Baby," 156–58;
   "Black Jesuz," 158
"Shall We Gather At the River," 82

"Sh-boom," 102
Shelton, Billy, 93
Shines, Johnny, 92
"Shining Star," 145
"Shout!" 29, 30, 32
shout, the: in black worship, 17, 22,
    102 116; depiction in "Shout!"
    31–32; influence on rhythm &
    blues, 33; and Sun Ra, 141. *See
    also* ring shout, holy dance
"Shoutin' in the Amen Corner," 78
Shuffle Along, 114
Silhouettes, 93
"Sing a Song," 145
"Sing, You Sinners!" 75, 77
"Sittin' on a Log," 60
Sixteenth Street Baptist Church, 121
Smith, Bessie, 10, 25, 27, 166 n 35
Smith, Fred, 109
Smith, Grafton Elliot, 139
Smith, Mamie, 25
Solar-Hieroglyphics Arkestra, 140.
    See also Arkestra; Cosmic Space
    Jazz Group; Intergalactic
    Research Arkestra; Astro-Solar
    Arkestra
Solomon's Temple, 124
"Somebody Told Me," 136
soul charts, 129
Soul Stirrers, 84, 89, 105, 106, 108
"Southern Can Is Mine," 49–50
space traveler imagery (in funk), 138
Spaniels, 93, 139
Spartanburg Famous Four, 77
Specialty Records, 95, 109
speaking in tongues, 8, 16, 19, 22,
    70. *See also* glossolalia
speech-song of the black preacher,
    70, 125–26, 135
"Spend the Night," 134
spirit possession: in West-African
    religion, 4–5, 18, 21–22; in black
    Christian worship, 22, 33, 66, 94,
    110; and religious stereotypes,
    102–3; and the slave preacher,
    115. *See also* Holy Spirit

possession, West-African
    worldview
Spirituals to Swing Concert, 166 n
    35
"Stand by Me," 104
"Stand by Me, Father," 104
Staples, Mavis, 127, 130
Staples, Pop, 130
Staple Singers, 110, 112, 127, 128,
    130
Stax, 31
Stevens, Vol, 43, 45
Still, William Grant, 101
"St. Louis Blues," 35
Stokes, Frank, 54, 65
Stoller, Mike, 63, 163 n 3.2
"Stonewall Blues," 43–44
storefront churches, 68–70
Storey, Charlie, 106
"Strange Things Happening Every-
    day," 84–85
Sun Ra, 138–41, 143. *See also*
    Blount, Herman
"Surely, God Is Able," 107
Sweet Sweetback's Baadasssss Song,
    151
"Swing Low, Sweet Chariot," 141–
    42

Taylor, Zola, 93, 165 n 10
Tharpe, Rosetta, 34, 82–84, 120, 166
    n 35
"That's Heaven to Me," 105–6
"That's the Way of the World," 145–
    46
"This World Is Not My Home," 141
Thornton, Willie Mae "Big Mama,"
    94, 163 n 3.2
"Too High," 131
"Too Much, Too Little, Too Late," x
Torey, George, 44–45
Traveling Soul Spiritualist Church
    (Chicago), 112, 122
Treemonisha, 59
"Trip to a Nigga Meeting," 71
"Truly Blessed," 136

Turner, Tina, 12, 28–29
"Turn Off the Lights," 134
Turpin, Thomas, 25
"Twelves, The," 46–47
Tympani Five, 28

"Unconditional Love," 156, 158
"Up on the Roof," 163 n 3.2
Utica Institute Jubilee Singers, 77

Vee Jay (records), 95, 110

Wallace, Christopher, 154. *See also* Biggie Small
"Wake Up Everybody," 136
Ward, Billy, 93
Ward, Clara, 107
Washington, Dinah, 12, 92, 95–97, 165 n 17. *See also* Ruth Lee Jones
Watson, Ivory "Deek," 86
Watson, John, 16, 19
Watson, Johnny, 113. *See also* Pitts, Reverend Alfred
Watts riot, 121
WDIA, 97
Webb, Chick, 28
"We're a Winner," 122

West-African worldview, 1–5. *See also* spirit possession
"What a Difference a Day Makes," 165 n 17
What's Going On, 129–30, 151
"When the Saints Go Marching In," 85–86
White, Joshua, 114. *See also* Pinewood Tom
White, Maurice, 143–46, 168 n 51
Wilkins, Reverend Robert, 34, 113. *See also* Tim Wilkins
Wilkins, Tim, 113. *See also* Wilkins, Reverend Robert
Williams, Bert, 74–75, 159
Williams, Deniece, x-xi, 33, 162 n 28
Williams, Joe, 41, 47–48, 51
Williams, Reverend Johnny, 114
Wilson, Kid Wesley, 52–53
Wonder, Stevie, 12, 127, 128, 131–33, 145
Wood, Randy, 110

"You Got to Go Down," 55
"You're Good for Me," 126
"You Send Me," 103, 106
"You Shall," 54, 65